Edith Cavell - Brussels via Yorc

By the author of
Jack the Ripper – Blood lines

Edith Cavell
Brussels via Yorc

A digest of the resistance movement in Belgium and France during the early part of the First World War

Anthony J Randall

Proofreading
www.folioproofreading.co.uk

First published in the United Kingdom in 2015
by The Cloister House Press

ISBN 978-1-909465-38-1

FOREWORD

I live on the North Norfolk coast and attended college just south of Norwich, in that same county. The village of Swardeston lies less than two miles south of Keswick College and played a significant part in my learning to love this part of the country.

Swardeston was the birth place of Edith Cavell and a small monument is positioned at the entrance to the Parish Church where her father was the vicar. Other monuments to her can be found in Norwich and in London.

My wife's aunt, Miriam Simpson, was born in 1910 and worked as nurse in Norfolk for most of her life. She spoke often of Edith Cavell's story and of her legacy. I feel that it is no exaggeration to say that Miriam felt inspired by her example. It is to Miriam that I dedicate this work.

Anthony J Randall

Sheringham, Norfolk

Edith Cavell

CONTENTS

ILLUSTRATIONS

To the Simpson Family - truly a Norfolk family

POLITICIANS AND ARMIES

THE GERMAN CONFEDERATION

The roots and causes of the Great War are as numerous and disputed as are those of its consequences and legacies. The unification of Germany under Bismarck provides a suitable point in time from which to begin and to understand not only the causes of the Great War but also why it was fought in the way it was.

In 1860 Prussia and Austria, just two of the states which constituted the German Confederation, were of similar size to one-another and together probably constituted two-thirds to three-quarters of the total land area of the entire confederation. Other states within the confederation were very much minor players and were insufficiently powerful to contend the will of Prussia and Austria, the latter exercising a stronger influence than did Prussia.

Otto von Bismarck was appointed Prime Minister of Prussia in 1862 and also took on the role of Foreign Minister, having served eleven years in foreign affairs as ambassador to Russia and later to France. Before that, he had been Prussia's representative at the federal Diet in Frankfurt. It was during his eight years in Frankfurt that Bismarck's antipathy to Austria and to its dominance of the German Confederation began to take form.

Bismarck, against the expectations of Emperor William I, opposed the emperor's desire for an ever-increasing military budget. Stalemate was anticipated but Bismarck interpreted this as permitting the continuation, ad infinitum, of the existing budget arrangements. Far from opposing a military build-up, he was able to make military reforms without the necessity to make reference to Parliament. The reforms allowed him to turn his attention towards foreign policy and take the first steps towards a united Germany under Prussia.

A brief war against Denmark over the duchies of Schleswig and Holstein left Prussia and Austria, rather than the German Confederation, dictating German interests, following which, Bismarck began fostering discord against Austria. In 1886 Prussia invaded Holstein, which was under Austrian influence following the war against Denmark, and very soon Prussia secured war with Austria, Saxony, Hesse-Kassel and Hanover. Having defeated Austria at Königgrätz, further conflict was suspended in the hopes that other European powers would not intervene, and the 'Peace of Nikolsburg' was concluded. In that settlement, Hanover, Hesse-Kassel, Nassau and Frankfurt were annexed by Prussia, which then became the dominant power in central Europe.

The North German Confederation, with Prussia dominant, was established in 1897 but Bismarck's attempts to persuade the southern German states to enter into closer union were unsuccessful. The southern states were finally persuaded to join those in the north after France declared war on Prussia in 1870 following a dispute over Prince Leopold of Hohenzollern-Sigmaringen being offered the Spanish throne; a dispute that Bismarck engineered and manipulated. France was defeated and Alsace and part of Lorraine, two French provinces with large German speaking populations, were annexed by Germany. French hostility towards Germany was firmly established. Austria was isolated from the rest of the German speaking Europe, looking east toward the Balkans. However, the 1879 accord between Germany and Austria-Hungary ensured some level of stability between the two, with a degree of mutual support, should either be attacked by Russia or France. This 'Dual Alliance' was increased to a 'Triple Alliance' with the addition of Italy in 1881.

ASSASSINATION IN SERBIA

In 1892 France and Russia entered into an agreement specifically intended to counteract the threat of the German, Austria-Hungarian and Italian 'Triple Alliance'. Britain had largely remained outside this tangle of inter-related treaties and alliances but in 1904 signed the 'Entente Cordiale' with France and in 1907 something similar with Russia. These agreements, moral rather than military, constituted the three-fold alliance that still bound Britain, France and Russia together at the outbreak of the Great War. Both Russia and Britain entered into much smaller alliances, although each with devastating implications for 1914: Russia to defend Serbia and Britain to defend Belgium.

During 1912 and 1913 Turkey was at war in the Balkans with Greece, Serbia, Bulgaria and Montenegro. Through the ensuing peace the smaller nations, under Turkish or Austro-Hungarian rule, experienced an increase in nationalistic fervour and demands.

Archduke Franz Ferdinand, nephew of Emperor Franz Josef and heir to the Austro-Hungarian Empire, was visiting Serbia with his wife Sophie in June 1914. On the 28th they were touring Sarajevo in an open car when Serbian nationalist Nedjelko Cabrinovic threw a bomb at their car; it rolled off the back of the vehicle, wounding an officer and some bystanders. Later that day, on the way to visit the injured officer, the archduke's procession took a wrong turn, and a second nationalist, Gavrilo Princip, saw his opportunity and fired into the car, shooting

Franz Ferdinand and Sophie at point-blank range. Franz Ferdinand and Sophie both died within the hour.

The assassination of the heir to the Austro-Hungarian Empire and his wife produced widespread shock across Europe. Austria-Hungary and Germany demanded that Serbia should open an investigation, but the Serbian Ministry of Foreign Affairs replied that "*Nothing had been done so far and that the matter did not concern the Serbian Government*". Austria-Hungary reminded Serbia, in the 'July Ultimatum', of its obligations to maintain good neighbourly relations and made specific demands to prevent the publication of propaganda advocating the violent destruction of Austria-Hungary. Although Serbia made some concessions, Austria-Hungary was not satisfied.

The next day, Serbian reservists crossed onto the Austro-Hungarian side of the Danube, and Austro-Hungarian soldiers fired into the air to warn them off, but the report to Emperor Franz-Joseph was of "*a considerable skirmish*". Austria-Hungary then declared war. Under the Secret Treaty of 1892, Russia and France were obliged to mobilise their armies if any of the Triple Alliance mobilised. The tensions and fears between the 'five powers' increased over the weeks, and Russian troops were mobilised along Germany's eastern border. Germany also feared invasion from France in the west.

Germany, bound by treaty to Austria-Hungary, declared war on Russia. France, bound by treaty to Russia, declared war on Germany and Austria-Hungary.

INVASION OF BELGIUM

Germany then implemented the so-called 'Schlieffen Plan'. Instead of aiming the first strike against Russia, the 'Schlieffen Plan' called for a

decisive debilitating blow at France through Belgium, rather than directly across the heavily fortified border between Germany and France. This plan was based upon the assumption that Russia would take six weeks in order to fully mobilise, and that, during such period, Germany could deliver a devastating blow to France before then turning east and facing Russia.

King Albert of Belgium denied German troops passage through Belgium, and called upon Britain to honour its promises made in various treaties with regard to enforcing Belgium's neutrality. On Monday 3rd August Sir Edward Grey, the British Foreign Secretary, made a speech to the British parliament:

> *If Belgium is compelled to submit to allow her neutrality to be violated, of course the situation is clear. Even if by agreement she admitted the violation of her neutrality, it is clear she could only do so under duress. The smaller states in that region of Europe ask but one thing. Their one*

> *desire is that they should be left alone and independent. The one thing they fear is, I think, not so much that their integrity but that their independence should be interfered with. If in this war, which is before Europe, the neutrality of those countries is violated, if the troops of one of the combatants violate its neutrality and no action be taken to resent it, at the end of war, whatever the integrity may be, the independence will be gone.*

Later in the day:

> *Germany sent yesterday evening at seven o'clock a note proposing to Belgium friendly neutrality, covering free passage on Belgian territory, and promising maintenance of independence of the kingdom and possession at the conclusion of peace, and threatening, in case of refusal, to treat Belgium as an enemy. A time limit of twelve hours was fixed for the reply. The Belgians have answered that an attack on their neutrality would be a flagrant violation of the rights of nations, and that to accept the German proposal would be to sacrifice the honour of a nation. Conscious of its duty, Belgium is finally resolved to repel aggression by all possible means. Of course, I can only say that the Government are prepared to take into grave consideration the information which they have received.*

On the 4th August, in response to German forces having crossed the border into his country, King Albert addressed the Belgian Parliament. In that address he spoke of Belgium's need of an "*autonomous existence*" and a duty to "*resist the invasion*" and warned that the enemy would find the Belgian people "*armed and resolved upon the greatest sacrifices*".

The British Foreign Office issued a statement late on the evening of 4th August:

> *Owing to the summary rejection by the German Government of the request made by His Majesty's Government for assurances that the neutrality of Belgium would be respected, His Majesty's Ambassador in Berlin has received his passport, and His Majesty's Government has declared to the German Government that a state of war exists between Great Britain and Germany as from 11pm on August 4.*

The British Expeditionary Force was instructed to begin mobilisation immediately and was fully prepared by Monday 17th August. Once they arrived in France, the British began moving towards the border with Belgium. The original intention was that the British Expeditionary Force should assemble at Le Cateau and Maubeuge and then take up position on the French left flank. Britain saw that this invasion of France through Belgium could destroy the French army, encircle the British Expeditionary Force and decimate it. The plan was now that the British and French should advance together and drive the Germans back out of Belgium, although the French were informed that the British could not be in place before the 24th August.

German troops entered Brussels in the early hours of 20th August. The British Expeditionary Force arrived in Bavay on Friday 21st August. Reginald and Marie de Croy met them there and then motored back to their château: the Château de Bellignies, where they met a company of the Middlesex Regiment who were to be billeted with them. The de Croys were actually an aristocratic family: Princess Marie Elisabeth de Croy et Solre born London 1875; Prince Léopold Marie Charles Edouard Emmanuel de Croy et Solre born San Remo 1877; Prince Reginald Charles de Croy et Solre born London 1878. Their father,

Alfred-Emmanuel de Croy, Prince of Croy and Solre, was born in Dülmen (Germany) 1842 and served for a time as Secretary of the Belgian legation in London. Their mother was Elizabeth Mary Parnell, the daughter of Hellyar Parnell who had bought the château which, in the past, had once belonged to the de Croy family.

German troops pushed on through Tirlemont, Gembloux, Aerschot, Malines and Louvain. The town of Louvain suffered particularly badly. Germans, to the rear of the advance, were attacked by Belgian forces advancing from Antwerp. German troops under fire withdrew to Louvain. Shots were heard, and the Allies were thought to be launching a major attack. No such attack was taking place, and the German authorities exacted revenge upon Louvain's citizens, who, they thought, had contrived the confusion that day. For five days the city was burnt and looted. Its library of ancient manuscripts was burnt and destroyed, along with many other public buildings. The population of Louvain was subject to mass shootings, regardless of age or gender. By 23rd August the town of Namur fell, and the battle of Mons began.

OCCUPATION OF BELGIUM

Sophie de Schaepdrijver describes the first impact of the German invasion of Belgium - the execution of civilians rounded up from villages surrounding their first obstacle, the ring of forts that circled Liège. Schaepdrijver writes that eight hundred and fifty civilians had been executed by the 8th August when Liège surrendered, most accused of being ‘franc-tireurs’ or civilian snipers, although this is generally believed to be wrongly claimed. Schaepdrijver observes that the massacres occurred where the invading army suffered setbacks, the German military not considering Belgium’s military defence to be legitimate. She also considers that the massacres went together with 'rituals' designed to demonstrate to civilians how helpless they were in the face of the German military; people being made to cheer the German troops; local dignitaries being publicly mistreated and in some cases being killed.

During this initial stage of invasion, the German military issued many orders and proclamations, often containing propaganda, to the Belgian civilian population. One of the earliest was by the German General Otto von Emmich:

> *It is to my very great regret that the German troops find themselves compelled to cross the Belgian frontier. They are acting under the constraints of an unavoidable necessity, Belgium's neutrality having been violated by French officers who, in disguise, crossed Belgian territory by motor-car in order to make their way into Germany.*

German army doctrine called for immediate and severe reprisals against any real or anticipated civilian resistance. It was argued that such 'schrecklichkeit' would end resistance quickly with relatively little bloodshed, whereas restraint would only encourage further resistance. The German high command expected to sweep through Belgium with negligible opposition, ordering that anything which delayed the German advance should be crushed mercilessly. Thus, the German military responded to any perceived act of resistance with harsh measures. Violence by German soldiers against Belgians, such as rape, was ignored or not seriously punished.

EARLY DAYS

EDITH CAVELL

In July 1914, a little after the assassination of Archduke Franz Ferdinand, Edith Cavell left Brussels for Norwich, the city in the east of England where her mother Louisa Cavell was celebrating her birthday on the 6th of that month. An annual holiday in Norfolk had become de-rigour for Miss Cavell, accompanied, in 1914, by Pauline Randall, one of two young English girls to whom she had become a 'surrogate'

parent and to whom she had given a home with her in Brussels. Edith Cavell was the matron of the Belgian School of Nursing in the Rue de la Culture and had also 'adopted' Grace Jemmett, both girls having had problems with their families, and both girls being given an opportunity to train as nurses.

The July holiday followed a familiar pattern. First to visit her mother at twenty-four College Road in Norwich, travelling just south of the city to meet family friends at Swardeston, where she had been born and where her father had once been vicar. As in previous years, rooms were taken with a Mrs. Harrison at Cumberland Cottage in West Runton for a two-week stay, the party travelling by train from Norwich and then arriving in West Runton by pony and trap from Sheringham. Towards the end of July, the two visitors returned to College Road. It was here that Edith Cavell received a telegram appraising her of the situation in Brussels and of the impending danger. The sender of the telegram was Millicent White, a sister at the nursing school, who, together with another sister, Elizabeth Wilkins, had been left in charge during the matron's absence.

Louise Thuliez makes mention of Edith Cavell's life before the war:

> *Miss Edith Cavell was born in Swardeston, in the county of Norfolk in 1866. her father, the Rev. Frederick cavell, was a man of lofty ideals and possessed a strict sense of duty [. . .] one can easily imagine the noble and somewhat severe education such a father gave to his daughter Edith and to her elder sister Florence . . .*
>
> *When Edith was about fifteen years old, she was sent to school in Brussels, after which she came back home to take up her old life beside her mother whom she idolised.*
>
> *At the age of twenty-two a legacy permitted her to take a trip to Switzerland. She went on into Bavaria where she entered a hospital as a volunteer nurse.*

At twenty-nine she entered the London Hospital where she went through her training . . . chosen to go to Maidstone where an epidemic of typhoid fever was raging . . . . returned to the 'London' [. . .] and a post at St Pancras Guardians at Highgate [. . .] In 1906 she accepted the superintendence of the Institut Berkendael (140 Rue de la Culture) which had been founded by Doctor Depage. . . .

The Nurses' Training-School was founded and the number of pupils increased from thirteen in 1907 to sixty in 1914. . . . as well as her training school she founded a surgical hospital and a sanatorium. To these she added some time later a 'crèche' with room for twenty-two babies.

Edith Cavell and Pauline Randall made a hasty return to Brussels and arrived at the nursing school in the Rue de la Culture in the early hours of 3rd August, before German forces crossed the border later on that same day. All Germans were ordered to leave Brussels, including the probationer nurses at the school, and many patients discharged themselves from hospital in order to distance themselves from the advancing German troops. Buildings, including the nursing school, flew the Red Cross flag and were prepared to treat the Belgian wounded. In fact the first to arrive were simply exhausted, and what injuries they did have were minor, resulting in rapid discharge back to their units.

Brussels was declared an 'undefended' city on 18th August, and the government, along with the King and Queen, relocated to Antwerp. The hope was that Brussels would not be subjected to the bombardment that Liège, Namur and Louvain had experienced. The civil population of Brussels made some attempts at defiance by digging trenches and erecting barricades, but they represented no real deterrent to the German army.

Just before midnight on the 19th August, the Germans arrived in Brussels. The civilian defence was ordered to disband, which they did, and the enemy began marching through the city in the direction of Paris, a procession that was to take two days to complete. On the afternoon of the second day, the Germans took possession of the Hôtel de Ville and raised the German flag. The occupation of Belgium was put under the direct control of Field-Marshal Baron von der Goltz Pasha, who exercised ruthless powers in combatting civilian resistance or dissent:

> *It is the stern necessity of war that the punishment for hostile acts falls not only on the guilty, but on the innocent as well [. . .] in the future, villages in the vicinity of places where railway and telegraph lines are destroyed will be punished without pity (whether they are guilty or not of the acts in question). With this in view hostages have been taken in all villages near the railway lines which are threatened by such attacks. Upon the first attempt to destroy lines of railway, telegraph or telephone, they will immediately be shot.*

Edith Cavell's L'École Belge d'Infirmières Diplômées, well prepared but under utilised by the German wounded, sent nurses to the Ambulance du Palais Royal, which operated under the Red Cross and treated the wounded of both sides. German attitudes to the 'ambulance' were suspicious and even hostile. Belgian, French and English wounded were dispatched to Germany once they had been 'patched-up', whatever their condition. All lines of communication were closed to the civilian population; no telephone, no post, no travel, whether by rail, by car or even by bicycle. Belgium was isolated from the entire world, except at tremendous risk to those who refused to observe the rules.

The German entry into Brussels also marked the beginning of censorship and control of the fourth line of communication: newspapers and their dissemination of information. The Belgian reaction to the prohibition and destruction of printing equipment was simply to organise the importation of other Belgian newspapers from Antwerp: foreign newspapers even, from Paris, Amsterdam or London, as well as books and pamphlets.

MARIE DE CROY

While Edith Cavell was visiting her mother in Norwich, Princess Marie Elisabeth de Croy et Solre was staying with friends in London. She also received a telegram, which advised her that if she planned to return home, then she should leave immediately. De Croy left London on the 1st August and took a ferry to Calais. She commented later that although the seriousness of the situation was not apparent to the native English population, Germans were leaving England 'en-masse' for the safety of their home country. From the French port Marie de Croy went by train to Valenciennes, where she was met by her brother Reginald and driven by car to the family home, the Château de Bellignies, close to Bavay. On the evening of her return home her eldest brother, Leopold, also arrived, having had a difficult journey south from Brussels, and before that, from his yachting vacation in Russia.

Like Edith Cavell in Brussels, Marie de Croy offered her home to the Red Cross and, in keeping with the family's aristocratic station, it was designated as a French hospital for officers. Bavay, to the south of Bellignies, was similarly organising to attend to the wounded; here the Red Cross took over the College of the Assumption.

The British Expeditionary Force, when it arrived 21st August, were detailed to guard and mine roads and bridges between Bavay and the

Belgian frontier. From comments made by Marie de Croy the British were without a sufficient number of maps and were supplementing their meagre supply with local motoring maps. During the run-up to the Battle of Mons, the château played host to Charles Fergusson commanding the 2nd Army Corps, Lord Graham and members of General French's staff.

The first of the retreating English to arrive at the château were exhausted, some wounded, some seriously injured. From time to time a doctor would arrive to help, but there was little that could be done except to prepare the serious cases for evacuation to Amiens, the less serious cases to the college in Bavay. Two such casualties taken to Bavay were Captain Preston, an artillery officer, and his companion, described by Marie de Croy as his driver. However, Captain Preston and two other officers, Lieutenants Marston and Moore, got left behind at Bavay when the hospital was evacuated the day after their arrival.

The first German troops arrived at the gates of the Château de Bellignies on the 25th August in the form of General von Kluck,

commander of the German First Army which had taken Brussels, who was accompanied by the Duke of Schleswig-Holstein, a grandson of Queen Victoria. The Duke interrogated the patients, "*dragging the bandages off our poor wounded men*", as Marie de Croy put it, "*with one man fainting from the pain of being made to stand on a recently 'set' broken leg*".

The following day, General von Kluck and the Duke of Schleswig-Holstein were replaced by General von Bauer and the Grand Duke of Mecklenburg-Strelitz. Tensions within the château eased at this point and the two sides' wounded began to spend time together both inside the château and in the grounds. However, the wounded from each side made efforts to not appear too ready to either return to active service or to be transported to prison camps.

LOUISE THULIEZ

In July 1914, while Edith Cavell and Marie de Croy were both holidaying in England, a young French schoolteacher named Louise Thuliez was spending her vacation in the small village of Saint-Waast-la-Vallée. At two in the afternoon of 2nd August, church bells were rung to announce that the anticipated German invasion was in progress. Louise Thuliez writes that by the 21st August troops of the British Expeditionary Force were heading north through Saint-Waast, heading for the Belgian border: two days later, those same troops were passing through Saint-Waast again, heading south and pursued by the Germans.

The English soldiers brought with them many casualties and, rather than move them on to the Red Cross hospital in Bavay, they were made as comfortable as possible in the Hôtel de Ville with a promise that transport would arrive the following morning to take the casualties on to safety. This was accomplished but, with insufficient transport, six of the wounded were left behind on the promise of more transport the following morning. By that following morning the Germans had taken control of Saint-Waast and the remaining casualties were marooned.

Occupation brought with it looting. The Germans, at first hesitant in isolation from their main force, became bold when they realised they would meet no armed resistance. Houses were broken into and all food and drink (wine and beer) was confiscated and immediately consumed by a tired and hungry army. Louise Thuliez describes these "warriors on horseback" making sport by dressing up in women's clothes they had stolen. She writes:

Mlle Louise Thuliez, décorée de la Légion d'honneur et de la Croix de guerre.

The wholesale pillage of the shops was carried out in a rapid and systematic manner, as though it was part of a soldier's work. It was organised thus. The soldiers inside passed the things through the windows to their comrades outside, who, in turn, caught them and handed them on to those on the wagons, who did the packing-up. The officers supervised the work with approving eyes. Evidently in the German military code, pillage is looked upon as a conqueror's right.

Henriette Moriamé, a friend of Louise Thuliez, offered accommodation for the casualties in her large house in the village and, once installed, their wounds were dressed. Shortly after this, German officers forced entry into the house and discovered the English soldiers. Again, the treatment of the injured was less than was required by the Geneva Convention, the bandages were removed and open wounds inspected. This was followed by what was described by Louise Thuliez as "*detailed and threatening interrogation*" of the men about the previous day's battle and the strength of the allied army. The two women were told that their English wounded were to be removed to the Red Cross hospital at Bavay but this never happened. The situation was later formalised when René Delame was ordered to make an inventory of all the English and French soldiers being treated in the various hospitals.

Food was a major problem for both the civilian population and for the casualties who were being given shelter. There was strict rationing of meat and bread, but local farmers were complicit in hiding and distributing supplies. A census was ordered of all livestock, and local farmers were obliged to hand over to the German authorities a significant portion of each beast slaughtered.

THE FOREST OF MORMAL

As the wounded recovered, Louise Thuliez and Henriette Moriamé made the conscious decision to become more pro-active in their opposition to the German occupation. In response to proclamations that all allied soldiers in hiding must give themselves up as prisoners and that failure to comply would mean severe penalties for them and others who offered them assistance, the two women decided to relocate them to more secure shelter.

Louise Thuliez writes that she and Henriette Moriamé went to see Reginald de Croy at the Château de Bellignies and asked him to find somewhere to shelter them. Marie de Croy recounts that the two girls arrived one afternoon, asking for Reginald, and that he agreed to help them. The forest of Mormal was close by and Reginald de Croy made arrangements with one of the 'cottagers' in the northern part of the forest, close to Obies, to take them in. This action was also a turning point for the de Croys in that they had also made the conscious decision to become pro-active in their 'resistance'.

The two girls spent the following day in collecting donations of civilian clothing for the soldiers, which they delivered that evening. At Saint Waast, the following day, they reported to the mayor that the soldiers had insisted on leaving Henriette Moriamé's house and that the girls were unable to stop them. This assertion that the soldiers had left without assistance, and without notice, meant that the mayor's position would be secure regarding any suggestion of collaboration.

It appears that local awareness of soldiers hiding in the forest became quite widespread, and 'strays' were commonly delivered to the château or information of their whereabouts given to the de Croys who then rounded them up and took them to the forest hiding place. Very shortly the numbers had grown to forty men who had been cut off in the retreat from Mons, and there was concern about the lack of security amongst the local population.

Reginald de Croy, Louise Thuliez, Henriette Moriamé and others began to make nightly 'trawls' through the forest and surrounding villages in search of more soldiers to be rescued. Often such journeys, on foot, could be twenty miles or more. Additionally the dead were buried and all possessions, such as pay-books, identity discs, photographs etc., retrieved and recorded for passing back to London and then on to grieving families.

CROSSING THE LINE

In Brussels two English soldiers, Lieutenant Colonel Dudley Boger and Company Sergeant Major Frank Meachin, were brought to the nursing school in Rue de la Culture by Albert Libiez of Wiheries in search of refuge for them. Edith Cavell took the two fugitives in: nursed them, found them civilian clothes, organised a 'safe house' in Avenue Louise and found guides to take them through to Holland. Before leaving the city, Dudley Boger gave written dispatches to Sister Millicent White at the Royal Palais Hospital; she was planning to smuggle herself out of Belgium into Holland and return to England. She reached London and the War Office four days later.

Jacqueline van Til, who had attended the two English soldiers, writes that the following day a further nine soldiers were delivered to the nursing school in the company of a French woman by the name of Mademoiselle Martin, who was in fact, she later discovered, Louise Thuliez.

Edith Cavell had now joined the 'resistance'. Perhaps not blowing up trains or killing German soldiers or sabotaging factories, but she certainly overstepped the boundaries of nursing and humanitarian assistance. She, Louise Thuliez, Henriette Moriamé, Reginald de Croy and Marie de Croy had well and truly 'crossed the line'.

CAPTAIN PRESTON

Reginald and Marie de Croy associated themselves closely with the hospital at Bavay, which was full of both English and French wounded. Marie de Croy writes that the hospital became a focal point for all the local authorities, such as the mayor, the notary and the heads of groups like the Red Cross. The de Croys, fluent in both French and English, acted as interpreters. It was on one of their visits that they met Captain Preston, whom Reginald de Croy had driven to Bavay just before the arrival at the Château de Bellignies of General von Kluck and the Duke of Schleswig-Holstein.

Captain Preston, his injuries healing, planned to escape. The de Croys offered him refuge at the château and promised to try to establish a safe route back to his own lines. A few days later he turned up at the château in the early hours of the morning, saying that the hospital had been taken over by the Germans with a heavy guard posted within the hospital as well as the town. Captain Preston was temporarily housed at the Château de Gussignies in the care of Baron René de Witte, before being taken back to the Château de Bellignies and into hiding in a secret part of the tower.

This tower was the oldest part of the Château de Bellignies, dating back to the Middle Ages. The walls are said to have been up to nine feet (2.75m) thick and contained a stairway. The entrance to the tower had been walled up some time previously but was opened up and made to appear as a cupboard, with an easily removed false back, which then served as a secret hiding place when needed. That part of the château was rarely used but had, at some time, been used as a hospital, so there were beds already installed.

The group of forty soldiers hiding in the Mormal forest near the village of Englefontaine were led by Lieutenant Bushell of the Queens Bays. This group made some attempts at sabotage on the railway line between Aulnoye and Landrecies but were unable to make much impact on the German army. However, they had drawn attention to themselves, and the Germans began a more focused search of the forest.

Louise Thuliez and Henriette Moriamé approached Captain Preston at the Château de Bellignies to inform him of the group of men at the Englefontaine camp. Captain Preston was anxious to be in communication with Lieutenant Bushell, and the two girls, now being referred to in code as the 'girl guides', journeyed between the two officers a number of times. Louise Thuliez writes that there was an intention to concentrate all allied troops in a single camp in the forest, from which to attempt a serious drive to get back through enemy lines.

The Germans pre-empted such a move by discovering and raiding the allied camp. Although no one was shot or captured, the entire group was scattered, and only twenty-three found their way back to the camp. Lieutenant Bushell and the men, now effectively under his command, crossed the forest in the direction of Obies, where the other camp was located, and formed a combined group. Louise Thuliez, upon becoming aware of the situation, took Captain Preston to meet with Lieutenant Bushell at Obies and returned that same night to the Château de Bellignies.

It was Captain Preston's wish that the combined group should relocate to the Château de Bellignies, from where it might be possible to launch an armed attack on the Germans and to force a way back through the lines to reach allied positions. Lieutenant Bushell was reluctant to move out of the forest but was eventually persuaded. All signs of the camp were destroyed and the entire party set out for the château in two groups: the first led by Henriette Moriamé and the second by Louise Thuliez. The journey took them from Obies, through Bermeries and Saint-Waast-la-Vallée, to Bellignies, probably about fifteen miles by fields, woods and back roads. Upon arrival, Lieutenant Bushell went to the château to billet with Captain Preston, while the remainder spent the night in the attic of the porter's lodge.

Over the following days it was decided that the men and non-commissioned officers should give themselves up to the Germans through the auspices of the Red Cross at Bavay. This was, in the main, in recognition of the danger that the local population would be in if the soldiers were to be discovered by the Germans. Again, Louise Thuliez and Henriette Moriamé guided them, and they were handed over to the mayor as the representative of the Red Cross. The Germans were not convinced that the men had been living rough in the forest since the Battle of Mons and imposed heavy fines on the local civilian population, against which the mayor was held hostage. Captain Preston and Lieutenant Bushell remained in hiding at the château.

JEANNE DE BELLEVILLE

At the end of November the de Croys were visited by the Countess Jeanne de Belleville, a French woman who lived just across the border in Belgium. With her she had her nephew, Eric de Belleville, who wanted to escape to Holland in order to join the French army. They left the following day for Brussels, and from there Eric succeeded in crossing the border into Holland. On her return, the Countess Jeanne de Belleville again visited the de Croys and reported that one of the group that was sent on from Brussels to Holland was an English major who had been sheltered and helped on his way by Edith Cavell.

Lieutenant Bushell and Captain Preston left the Château de Bellignies in the afternoon of the twenty-ninth of December in the company of Louise Thuliez and Charlotte Matha, a member of the de Croy household. The first leg of the journey was to Montignies-sur-Roc, the home of Countess Jeanne de Belleville and her mother, just across the Belgian border. The following morning the group, plus Jeanne de Belleville, travelled to Dour and left her to go on by tram to Mons, meeting Reginald de Croy by arrangement at the church of St. Waudru. The two Englishmen were supplied with false papers describing them as 'hairdresser's assistants'.

Their contact in Brussels was the Père de Longueville, who took them to the house of the Countess de Mevius, where they also met Countess Jeanne de Belleville, who stayed with them until they left Brussels for Holland, via Antwerp, guided by Père de Longueville. They eventually reached England and returned to active service: Captain Preston to Mesopotamia and Lieutenant Bushell back to France.

Early in the new year the last of the 'enemy' soldiers were evacuated from the hospital in Bavay. The two 'long term' English resident wounded at the Château de Bellignies were allowed to stay until they were fit enough to travel. Marie de Croy writes that the departure of these two men, Tom Hogg and George Goodier, was greatly delayed, during which time they assisted in the care of many refugees before finally being sent to prison camps in Germany until the end of the war.

It was agreed that Reginald de Croy, Jeanne de Belleville, Louise Thuliez and Henriette Moriamé should make concerted efforts to locate further English and French soldiers in need of assistance. Some of those located were taken to the Château de Bellignies and from there to Brussels and, amongst others, to Edith Cavell's clinique in the Rue de la Culture.

IN TOO DEEP

THE PASSWORD IS 'YORC'

Marie de Croy is quite explicit in reporting that Edith Cavell offered to house any men that Reginald de Croy should send en-route to Holland. In doing so it was agreed that, for security reasons, any men so dispatched should announce themselves as having been sent from Mr. 'Yorc' (the family name Croy reversed). Jacqueline Van Til, one of the nurses at Edith Cavell's clinique, writes that quite a number of English soldiers passed through their hands during January. Although no longer escorting soldiers personally, Reginald de Croy made regular visits to Edith Cavell in Brussels, as did Louise Thuliez.

Louise Thuliez writes that the roads crossing the Franco-Belgian frontier represented no great danger to the guides. The main roads were blocked by ditches filled with barbed wire, but side roads, easily enough followed by those with local knowledge, provided a safer route with minimal chance of meeting German patrols. From Bellignies the crossing took them to Arquenne and from there on to Brussels.

Travelling was a little easier in Belgium than in northern France. Belgian nationals were permitted free movement, provided they were able to provide their identity papers on demand: French nationals also needed a monthly permit to live or work in Belgium. Thus, a growing number of French soldiers, separated from their units, found their way back behind their own lines by travelling through Belgium to Holland and thence back to France.

German propaganda was distributed in the form of strictly censored newspapers, such as *La Belgique' Le Bruxellois*, *La Gazette des Ardennes* and *La Gazette de Lorraine*. By early January the French 'resistance', if one may refer to them as such, countered this with *Le Journal des Occupés ... Inoccupés*, changing its name later to *L'Oiseau de France*. By the end of January there was a Belgian equivalent *La Libre Belgique,* and it was the clandestine distribution of this newspaper for which Philippe Baucq was to lose his life.

REGINALD DE CROY

Reginald de Croy continued to make regular trips between Bellignies and Brussels, bringing back with him copies of the clandestine pamphlets and newspapers, which he distributed among the local French population in order to boost morale. Together with other strategic intelligence collected by guides and helpers, the accumulated information represented a useful aid to the British and French forces. The information was smuggled out along with the repatriated soldiers.

As time went by, it became obvious that the Germans were suspicious of the activities in and around the Château de Bellignies and of the de Croys and their immediate circle. Reginald de Croy was finding that it was taking longer, and a great deal of persuasion, to get his travelling permit for Belgium. Funds to support the guides, for soldiers' food and lodgings, for identity papers etc., were getting very low, and Reginald de Croy made further trips into Belgium and through Holland, into France and even England, to try to get an allocation of funds from the army to cover those needs. Specifically, they were aware that Edith Cavell, in the Rue de la Culture, had spent all her own money and even some which belonged to L'ecole Belge pour les Infirmières Diplomées.

While Reginald de Croy was away, towards the end of March, the Château de Bellignies was raided by a party of more than forty German soldiers, armed with a search warrant. There were sixteen English soldiers hiding in the château tower at the time. Despite a search lasting several hours, they remained undetected. However, it was quite obvious to the de Croys and the 'girl guides' that the Germans were suspicious, and these concerns were reinforced when 'safe' houses in Brussels began to be targeted and a procession of 'suspicious' visitors began to visit the Château de Bellignies.

Despite the risk of attracting attention from the Germans, Marie de Croy travelled to Brussels to consult with Edith Cavell on the recent developments. Once there, she stayed at the Hôtel Britannique in order, so she says, not to compromise her friends by accepting their hospitality. When she went, the following day, to the Rue de la Culture she first met with Elizabeth Wilkins the nursing sister. When she met with Edith Cavell, she told her that their resistance activities must cease immediately to which Cavell appeared much relieved.

UNDER SUSPICION

Edith Cavell confessed that the clinique had been raided the previous day and that, in a desperate attempt to hide any incriminating evidence, she had burnt not only her own papers but also those concerning the clinique. She seemed as concerned about her inability to account to Dr Depage for clinique funds as to her own safety. However, during further conversation, it was decided that the balance of men still hidden at the Château de Bellignies should be sent through to Holland, but that no more would be lodged at the clinique. Edith Cavell would continue to direct the guides and disseminate information on routes and schedules.

Marie de Croy and Charlotte Matha, who had accompanied her as far as Mons, had a difficult journey back to the Château de Bellignies. The guides continued to report greater and greater difficulties in crossing the Franco-Belgian frontier, and the Germans began installing electric fencing. It was becoming impossible to bribe the Landsturm, or militia, men to 'look the other way' – many of whom had already paid for their indiscretions with their lives.

When Reginald de Croy returned to the Château de Bellignies from his trip to Holland, and then England, he reported that he had secured new lodgings in Brussels, as an alternative to the clinique in the Rue de la

Culture. He also reported that while at the War Office in London he had met a group of twelve soldiers that had taken the route from Bellignies, via Edith Cavell in Brussels, and had reached London after a week in transit. While he was in London, a newspaper report about the escape of twelve British soldiers "*who had lain hidden in a château in the north of France and had arrived after a dangerous passage through Belgium*" had caught his eye. Although no names were mentioned, the details entirely compromised the efforts being made by the 'resistance' group. The British censors were informed and further such reports were suppressed; however, individual soldiers, upon reaching Holland, very often sent postcards back to Brussels, expressing sincere thanks without realising the possible consequences of their well intended actions.

It was during the early part of 1915 that Jeanne de Belleville, already working with the de Croys, met Hermann Capiau, a mining engineer living at Wasmes in the middle of the coal mining area, known as the 'Borinage', which lies between Mons and Charleroi. From the first arrival of the British Expeditionary Force in August 1914 he had offered assistance in guiding: firstly fighting troops advancing: secondly injured and separated troops retreating. Hermann Capiau had also taken care of British soldiers and had arranged for their repatriation via Belgium, using the clinique in Rue de la Culture, and had thus made the acquaintance of Edith Cavell. It was Hermann Capiau that first introduced Louise Thuliez to Edith Cavell, who, in turn, introduced her to Philippe Baucq.

GASTON QUIEN

In the early months, soldiers who crossed the frontier into Belgium were first handed over to Angelina Quinchon to await collection by Hermann

Capiau. He, in turn, housed them in miners' homes in the Borinage to await guides and documents. While numbers were few, an ad hoc process was quite possible, but as refugee numbers increased it became necessary to make the journey from Erquennes to Mons as a single group. Hermann Capiau organised the blank identity cards and Jeanne de Belleville the photographs and other details which needed to be added. Hermann Capiau then applied the 'official' stamp and he and his wife signed the identity cards using fictitious names.

Edith Cavell definitely felt herself under suspicion and under surveillance. She asked Jeanne de Belleville to "*tell all the helpers not to send any more men here for the present, as my situation is becoming more and more strained every day*". Accordingly, Philippe Baucq began to take on a larger and larger role in taking over responsibility from Edith Cavell.

The Germans were closing in, more and more arrests were made, and it was evident that the days of the group were numbered. Reginald de Croy left the Château de Bellignies for Brussels, from there to Holland and then England, not to return until after the end of the war.

Jacqueline Van Til says that she first encountered Georges Gaston Quien (she spells the name 'Quin') sometime in June 1915. While walking in the Rue de Berkendael, close to the clinique, she was approached by Quien, whom she describes as a tall handsome man with a most beautiful French accent and the manners of a well bred gentleman. She also describes him as having a 'Bourbon' nose, keen blue eyes, yet a soft and kindly expression.

Quien told Jacqueline Van Til that he was a French soldier and that he was looking for the Edith Cavell Clinique. Exercising a degree of caution, she directed him away from the clinique, but he followed her and then crossed the road to speak to a second man standing opposite the clinique, who then indicated towards Edith Cavell standing in the street outside. She and Pauline Randall went back inside the clinique, but the two men approached the door and were let in by Edith Cavell.

A few minutes later Edith Cavell introduced the two men to Jacqueline Van Til and asked her to take Quien to a room where there was a French soldier in residence. Quien's companion, an Englishman for whom no name was given to Jacqueline Van Til but who was referred to only as Mr X, was placed in a room where several English soldiers were talking and smoking together. There was a planned departure to Holland the following day, but Quien said that he did not feel well enough for the journey and it was agreed that he should stay behind. The others, including Mr X (referred to as Motte at Quien's court-marshal after the war), were taken by Edith Cavell to meet the guide, Victor Gilles.

It appears that Quien was able to charm the ladies of the clinique, and Jacqueline Van Til claims that all the nurses fell head-over-heels in love with him, as did Pauline Randall and Léonie, the cook's daughter. Jacqueline Van Til asserts that she was the sole exception to this affliction, but it must be remembered that she was writing in 1922, after all the facts were known.

The guide Gilles returned to the clinique a few days after the group had departed for Holland, to report that on reaching Antwerp the Englishman, Motte, had disappeared. Gilles told Edith Cavell that he thought Motte was a spy and that she should be very cautious with anyone who came to the clinique. That same evening a German officer arrived at the clinique to enquire about a vacant room for his son, who was very ill, but he behaved impeccably, did not ask to inspect the clinique, and left without speaking to anyone else.

The following day, having been asked to deliver a letter to Philippe Bancq, Jacqueline Van Til was met by Quien as she was walking along the Chaussée de Waterloo on the way to Philippe Bancq's house.

Quien offered to take her to a near-by café for a glass of wine, an invitation which she declined. She saw him a little later on at the Porte de Schaerbeek; he didn't approach her but she felt that she was being followed and, being cautious, decided not to deliver the letter but to go on to a friend's house and make the delivery the following day.

Gaston Quien did finally leave, bound for Holland, but on the 29th of July presented himself again at the clinique without explanation. He was given a bed for the night but left suddenly the following morning. It was at this time that Edith Cavell entrusted Quien with a package, containing special road maps of the frontier region, for him to deliver to a Madame Machiels the following day. When finally delivered, two of the maps were missing.

At the conclusion of her book, Jacqueline Van Til relates that at the end of the war the French showed the nurses photographs of Gaston Quien and of Motte, who they said was German rather than, as the nurses had thought, English. The photograph of Quien showed him with his hair shorn and in prison uniform.

ARREST AND IMPRISONMENT

When Louise Thuliez visited Philippe Baucq in Brussels at the end of July it was to arrange alternative accommodation for her charges. The clinique in Rue de la Culture was to be phased out of the operations in the hope that Edith Cavell, now coming under suspicion, would not incur the wrath of the Germans. There was much to discuss and it was arranged that Louise Thuliez would stay with Philippe Baucq and his wife. Louise Thuliez attended to other matters during the day and went to the Baucq house late that evening of the 31st July. The whole family were in residence, including their eleven and fourteen year old daughters, all employed in preparing copies of the *Libre Belgique* for distribution.

As the household was retiring, Philippe Baucq opened the front door to let their dog out for a run. At that moment the house was invaded by German soldiers who rushed in the front door and took possession of the entire house. After some initial questioning both Louise Thuliez and Philippe Baucq were taken to the police station in Rue de la Loi, told that they were 'under arrest' and then transferred to the prison at St. Gilles.

A few days later, on the 6th August, the Germans took control of the clinique in Rue de la Culture. Edith Cavell had been visited, and questioned, by a German officer concerning possible communications between the clinique and the War Office in London. Edith Cavell was interviewed in her office and then driven to the 'Commandantur', or German Headquarters, again in Rue de la Loi. Sister Wilkins was also taken away by the Germans but was allowed to return to the clinique about nine-o'clock that same evening. A few days later, Edith Cavell was also transferred to the prison at St. Gilles.

A week or so later, Jeanne de Belleville was also arrested and taken into custody by the Germans. Shortly after Jeanne de Belleville's arrest, Marie de Croy was visited by a German, pretending to be an escaped British prisoner, looking for a way to get back to England. Marie de Croy and Charlotte Matha were very suspicious and the two women exercised great caution. Otto Meyer, as he was later found to be, was advised to hand himself in to the German authorities as the de Croys had no way, and no intention, of aiding him.

Two days after Otto Meyer's visit, the Château de Bellignies was invaded by German soldiers seeking Reginald de Croy, who was, by then, in Brussels. Marie de Croy, without being specific, implied that he might possibly be in hiding at the de Croy's property at Solre-le-

Château. The Germans spent some days in trying to get information out of the estate's head keeper, named Legat and then some weeks imprisoning him in the belief that Legat, was supporting Reginald de Croy, who was hiding in the woods.

In Brussels, Reginald de Croy was with Marie de Lichtervelde at her house in the Avenue des Nerviens. While the two were discussing the situation, Reginald de Croy spotted Gaston Quien, someone that many of the 'inner circle' had reason to mistrust, in the street outside. This was the final development which convinced Reginald de Croy that he should make his escape, and, after consulting the eminent lawyer

Maître Alexandre Braun, embarked on the first stage of his journey to London.

The Germans kept the Château de Bellignies in isolation from the outside world for a few days following the initial takeover. Then Marie de Croy was taken to Brussels, nominally as a 'witness' but in reality as a prisoner at St. Gilles. During the journey she was subjected to a constant stream of questioning and was assured that 'the others', presumably Louise Thuliez, Philippe Baucq, Jeanne de Belleville and Edith Cavell, had made a clean breast of it and that she should do likewise.

INTERROGATION

At this stage in the occupation the governor and gaolers at the prison at St. Gilles were still Belgians but were under the supervision of the Germans. The interrogations were undertaken by Lieutenant Bergan from the Dusseldorf Police, head of Station B in the Rue de Berlaimont, and by Lieutenant Pinkhoff who had operated as a German spy in Paris before the war.

Louise Thuliez writes that she was without any legal representation during interrogation and that her statements were made in French, translated into German by Lieutenant Pinkhoff and typed by their clerk Neuhaus. The statements in German were translated back into French, with many damning inaccuracies, but she was required to sign her name to the German version - which she could not read.

Marie de Croy was also interrogated by Lieutenants Bergan and Pinkhoff and was told that, despite earlier promises, she was not going to be released as she was too deeply involved in the conspiracy. She was told that her brother Reginald de Croy had escaped to Holland, which, at the time, she did not know whether to believe or not, thinking that it might be a ploy to learn more from her.

A few days later Marie de Lichtervelde was allowed to visit under the strict watch of Lieutenant Bergan, who made the strict provision that they spoke only of family affairs and not of the matters under discussion. However, Marie de Lichtervelde did tell her that Maître Alexandre Braun would conduct her defence, but that at that time he was not able to learn with what offence she was to be charged.

During this time, between arrest and trial, Edith Cavell was kept isolated from the outside world. The staff at the clinique were particularly anxious to hear news of her, but they were reduced simply to wandering about the periphery of the prison at St. Gilles and petitioning the head warden for snippets of information. One or two letters were sent and replies received, but they contained nothing as to the state of her interrogation or information regarding the charges.

The nursing school had anticipated that their own lawyer, Maître Braun, would represent Edith Cavell in court, but the Germans would not accept him, so they appointed Maître Sadie Kirschen in his stead. However, shortly before the court date, the Germans then refused Maître Kirschen's appointment and appointed a German lawyer to represent her.

THE TRIAL

The trial began on 7th October in the Belgian Senate, which was to be used as a court. The accused, thirty-five in all, were together for the first time, and it was only at this point that each was aware of which others had been similarly accused. Once the formalities of swearing in the judges were completed, the prisoners with major charges to answer were removed from the court, but those facing lesser charges were allowed to remain throughout the trial.

Edith Cavell was the first to be questioned. Louise Thuliez describes the cross-examination of Edith Cavell as a 'mockery', being simply a summing up of all the questions that had been asked of her during the police enquiry, with no opportunity to bring fresh matters to the court's attention. The trial was conducted in German, with translation by the court official, which by no means helped to make things clear. Louise Thuliez also mentions that Edith Cavell's decision not to wear her nurse's uniform for the trial disappointed the other defendants. Marie de Croy writes that this was the first time that she had ever seen Edith Cavell out of her nurse's costume. Her defence amounted to a statement that she had simply done what she thought was her duty in saving the lives of men whom she knew were in imminent danger of death.

Louise Thuliez was asked about communications from the men she had helped to escape to Holland and the structure of the organisation of which she was a member. She felt that the Germans wanted to prove that they were an organised group, with a leader, and they questioned her regarding the guides, passports, official papers etc.. When asked what her motives were in doing this work, she replied "*Because I am a French-woman*".

Philippe Baucq was the third to be questioned, but there is little recorded as to his answers. However, Marie de Croy noted that he made copious notes during the trial, but, even though he was allowed to question the court on occasions, his statements or questions were virtually ignored. After him the rest of the defendants went through a similar process.

When it came to Marie de Croy to be examined, the first question was to establish that she was the sister of Reginald de Croy; he, of course having avoided arrest. She had been instructed by Maître Alexandre Braun to lay the culpability entirely on Reginald de Croy, well outside the reach of the German court.

Lieutenant Bergan, giving evidence, said that all the defendants were members of one organised band, which worked in two groups, and named Reginald and Marie de Croy, Herman Capiau, Georges Derveau, Jeanne de Belleville and Louise Thuliez as being the leaders in northern France. The operations around Mons were put down to Albert Libiez with many of the other accused.

The summing-up by the Military Prosecutor was basically to emphasise that the accused were all members of an organised group and guilty of 'high treason' and he demanded the death penalty for Philippe Baucq, Edith Cavell, Louise Thuliez, Louis Séverin, Jeanne de Belleville, Ada Bodart, Albert Libiez and Herman Capiau. The defence lawyers, having been given access neither to their clients nor to the evidence to be presented, were able to offer very little in the way of argument. The accused were returned to the prison at St. Gilles, being told that the sentence would be communicated to them later.

SENTENCE AND EXECUTION

On the afternoon of 11th October the accused were assembled in the central hall of the prison, and the Military Prosecutor read out the verdicts in German, which were then translated into French. Philippe Baucq, Louise Thuliez, Edith Cavell, Louis Séverin and Jeanne de Belleville were all sentenced to death. Herman Capiau, Ada Bodart, Albert Libiez and Georges Derveau were sentenced to fifteen years' hard labour and Marie de Croy to ten years' hard labour. Seventeen others were given sentences of between two and eight years and eight others were acquitted.

About seven o'clock that evening Mr Van Alteren, who had initially hoped to represent Edith Cavell in court, visited the clinique in Rue de La Culture and told the nurses that Edith Cavell was due to be executed the following morning at five o'clock. Some of the nurses from the clinique stood outside the prison at St. Gilles from four o'clock in the morning, saw two cars leave at five o'clock but could not see the occupants. The cars took Edith Cavell and Philippe Baucq to the 'Tir National', or rifle range, where they were to be executed.

The two were each stood against a white post, bound, with their eyes covered. On the command to fire the two shooting parties, eight men in each, let go a volley from six paces. Death was instantaneous. Dr. Benn certified that they were both dead. Soldiers unbound the bodies from the posts, placed them in the coffins which had been lying close by the posts and then straight into the already dug graves.

News of the executions reached the other prisoners on the following day via the German chaplain celebrating Holy Communion. However, the general population heard the news on the morning of the twelfth, the day of the executions. A proclamation was 'placarded' on the walls of Brussels, which named those who had been sentenced and stated that the executions of Edith Cavell and Philippe Baucq had already taken place. The proclamation was signed by General Von Bissing, the German governor of Brussels, with the added comment that the facts were being placed before the public as "*a solemn warning*".

Two weeks after the executions, the other prisoners who were given the death penalty received a visit from the Marquis de Villalobar, the Spanish Ambassador in Brussels. He told them each, in separate interviews, that their death sentences had been commuted. There appears to have been some efforts by the Germans to hide the French nationality of the prisoners, and it was the intersession of the King of Spain, with other influential people on behalf of the Belgians, that secured their reprieve. On 8th November it was announced by the Germans that the Kaiser had 'deigned' to commute the sentences of death to '*hard labour for life*".

The American embassy had also been working behind the scenes to secure reprieves, initially for Edith Cavell, despite the Germans acting with such haste that an effective campaign was very difficult. Further efforts on behalf of the others were made via the Spanish Ambassador. The prime force in this endeavour was Hugh Gibson of the American Legation in Brussels. Unfortunately the American Minister, Brand Whitlock, was unwell and was assured that sentences would not be handed down, and certainly not implemented, as quickly as they proved to be. He did write a letter to General Von Bissing, explaining that he was too unwell to appeal in person.

THE FOREST OF MORMAL

BEHIND ENEMY LINES

Based at Maroilles, Salesches, Romeries, Solesmes and Obies, there appears to have been five distinct groups to the south of Mons, which began, very soon after the start of the retreat, to organise relief for British and French soldiers cut off behind enemy lines. One such soldier was Claude Henry Bushell, from Claro in North Yorkshire, a lieutenant in the Queen's Bays (2nd Dragoon Guards).

On the afternoon of 26th August, Bushell was acting as a 'galloper' or messenger, taking instructions to the 11th Hussars for them to fall back to Saint Quentin. Having delivered the instructions to their headquarters, Bushell then rode forward to directly notify the various patrols. Near the village of Escaufort, just south of La Cateau, he found himself behind enemy lines and surrounded by Germans. He turned his horse loose and took refuge in a culvert at the bottom of a railway embankment.

Bushell was trapped in his hiding place for three days, while the density of German soldiers remained too high to effect an escape. During that time Bushell survived without food or drink. When he was able to leave his hiding place, he made his way to the small village of Honnechy and approached a farmer's cottage, where he was fed and watered. However, while he was in the cottage, he was warned that the Germans were approaching, and he was forced to take refuge in nearby undergrowth.

Having spent the night in the open, he was then told of three other soldiers hiding in a nearby wood. Borrowing civilian clothes, which he put on over his uniform, he went with a local guide to find them. In fact there was a group of eleven men of the 11th Hussars in hiding, including a Sergeant Taylor, but no officer. René Delame describes the men as being in a poor condition and says that Bushell immediately took command. The soldiers had some assistance from the mayor of Honnechy, who provisioned them, but were unable to leave their hiding place for a further six days because of increased local German activity.

Bushell mobilised the group once things quietened down, and the group set out one evening with the intention of reaching Englefontaine by the following morning - this being the first leg of a march that should eventually end at Lille, where they would rejoin the British Expeditionary Force. Again, their progress was interrupted by German activity, and they were forced to take refuge in an abandoned hut on the edge of the Mormal forest.

The 'Forêt de Mormal', state owned, employed a Monsieur Taisne, described by René Delame as a warden, and by Louise Thuliez as a gamekeeper. Either way, Monsieur Taisne was obviously very familiar with the forest and very soon became aware of the English soldiers hiding there. Taisne, his friend and fellow patriot Alfred Rousseau and Rousseau's sister-in-law Mlle Regnier took on the task of provisioning the camp. As time went on more and more men joined Bushell's group near Englefontaine.

A rather interesting aside by Louise Thuliez refers to the Germans felling large numbers of trees in the forest, even establishing a new saw-mill for the purpose, and converting them into planks for the German front-line trenches. Somewhat whimsically, she mentions that transporting the planks from the saw-mill to the waiting wagons was undertaken by an elephant, perhaps liberated from a Belgian circus?

By the end of October, after nearly two months in hiding, the forest camp numbered forty men, still with a single officer, Lieutenant Bushell of the Queen's Bays. The men, English, Scottish and Irish, were from five different units. They had built themselves a hut deeper into the forest and, under the instructions of Monsieur Taisne, were confining themselves to the forest rather than venturing into the villages.

At about this time Louise Thuliez and Henriette Moriamé were looking for a refuge in the Mormal Forest where they could hide a group of six English soldiers to whom they had been giving sanctuary in Saint-Waast. Arriving at Landrecies, Thuliez learnt of the forty-strong group hiding in the forest, and they were introduced to Monsieur Taisne and his colleagues, who agreed to take them to meet Lieutenant Bushell.

What they found at the forest camp was a group of men living like outlaws and constantly under the threat of discovery, arrest and immediate execution. They had very little in the way of weapons and ammunition, and relied on the local population for food and news of the outside world. This nerve-racking existence led to imprudence on the part of the soldiers and carelessness on the part of the local villagers, who were threatened with immediate death if found supporting the 'enemy'. It seems that Monsieur Taisne fought a constant battle to keep these 'stir-crazy' men from exposing themselves to the risk of detection by the Germans, including painting an arrow on one of the trees with the words "*to the camp*".

ATTACK ON THE RAILWAY

Louise Thuliez makes a passing reference to an attempt by Bushell's group to blow up part of the railway line between Aulnoye and Landrecies: an attempt that failed but that also served to convince the Germans that there were significant numbers of English soldiers hiding in the forest. Thuliez describes this attempt in approving terms, René Delame gives a little more detail but describes it in less glowing terms.

According to Delame, the plan was initiated by a French officer who had approached the group hiding in the forest, saying that he had been given the task of blowing up the bridge at Wassigny. It appears that Monsieur Taisne was not convinced by this French officer but could not persuade Lieutenant Bushell (who promised help in the mission) that he might be an 'agent provocateur', trying to lure the soldiers out of the forest to be arrested by the Germans. Taisne, along with Messieurs Cousin and Labbé, visited the French officer at the forest camp, where Labbé recognised him as a Monsieur Leclercq from Briastre near Solesmes.

Despite opposition from Taisne, Cousin and Labbé, the entire group set out at dusk to meet up with Leclercq, then went on to reach Locquignol by about ten-thirty that evening. Leclercq's plan was that the group should attack the nearby German post at Hachette in order to obtain more arms and ammunition to supplement the single Mauser rifle carried by Leclercq and one other weapon which the group possessed. Taisne was against the attack, fearing a trap, but Bushell pressed on with ten of his men, ran into stiff opposition and retreated to the forest. Monsieur Leclercq was not seen again.

Before returning to Saint-Waast-la-Vallée, the two 'girl guides' left what little money they had with Lieutenant Bushell and gave him detailed directions on how to reach another, smaller, group of soldiers, which the two girls supported near Obies, located about ten kilometres north of their present camp. It was decided that if it became necessary to move camp, then they should join the other camp at Obies.

DEEP IN THE FOREST

Captain Preston, in hiding at the Château de Bellignies with Reginald and Marie de Croy, was told about the large group of men, led by Lieutenant Bushell, hiding in the south of the forest near Englefontaine. Preston was very anxious to get into communication with Bushell, so Louise Thuliez and Henriette Moriamé made a number of journeys between Bavay and the camp, carrying messages between the two officers. Marie Croy writes that Preston had some notion of amalgamating all the hidden groups into a single unit, able to fight its way through to Lille, where, he believed French and English troops were to be found. It was decided that Marie de Croy should take a trip deep into the forest in order to make direct contact with Bushell.

The de Croys had been left with an old mare, whose age had spared her from being commandeered by the Germans, which was harnessed to a small dog cart. Taking some provisions and a number of English language books, she and Mlle. Carpentier, sister of one of the local brewers and someone who had previously given support to stranded soldiers, set off from Bellignies for the Forest of Mormal.

Despite being simply dressed, the two women and their dog-cart drew much attention. They stopped at a cottage en route and persuaded the owner to take in their mare and dog cart and lend them a rather unkempt donkey and cart for the remainder of the journey. Even so, the pair were stopped by a patrol, but Marie de Croy was able to speak to them in German and pass unhindered. After several hours the pair reached the village of Englefontaine which Marie de Croy described as "*one long rambling street surrounded by woods*".

On reaching Englefontaine they learnt that the camp had again been forced to move deeper into the forest. The Chanoine Flament (in English, Canon) arranged for them to meet a young local girl who knew the location of the relocated camp. Despite having promised her father not to risk being shot, by making further visits to the camp, she agreed to guide the two women, and all three set out through the forest on foot. On their way they met German officers out shooting for sport but were allowed to continue unhampered, a particular relief as Marie de Croy was carrying letters and even cartridges.

At a point where the undergrowth was particularly thick, the young guide, followed by her companions, struck off down a scarcely visible track and after some time stopped where a piece of twine was strung between the branches. Touching the twine, a small bell rang and a British soldier met them. Following him further into the undergrowth, they reached a clearing, where they met Lieutenant Bushell, immaculately dressed in his army uniform.

René Delame, Marie de Croy and Louise Thuliez all write about Lieutenant Bushell's command of the disparate group of English, Scottish, Irish and French soldiers living rough in the forest. Discipline was maintained, and a sense of camaraderie was evident in the design and state of readiness of the camp, which had been developed into an underground facility, well camouflaged with woodland vegetation. Security was Bushell's primary concern, and his primary request to Marie de Croy was for arms and ammunition with which to defend themselves.

Marie de Croy, Mlle. Carpentier and their young guide returned to Chanoine Flament's house, arranged for a schedule of provisioning for the soldiers, and from there the Bellignies women returned to the château and Captain Preston.

THE CAMP IS FOUND

In the very early days of November the Germans, certain now that there was a significant number of fugitives hiding in the forest, began to increase their efforts in mounting more and more thorough searches. The Germans appear to have had information about the location of the camp because, at about noon, they arrived in strength to take soldiers by surprise. As it happens, only half the men were in the camp, the other half being about a kilometre away, just starting the afternoon shift building a new camp. The morning shift had just returned, but were warned of the Germans' approach by the noise they made in crashing through the undergrowth. The British sentry gave the alarm, and the soldiers fled into the forest.

That evening, a number of the fugitives returned to the camp in the hope of retrieving provisions and weapons. The Germans were still there, lying in wait, and at the first sounds of men approaching they opened fire. There were no injuries but the men were scattered far and wide, only twenty-two finding their way back to the new site and Lieutenant Bushell. Survival in the forest was now impossible, and Bushell, with his band of twenty-two, set off for Obies as directed by

Louise Thuliez, who writes that they were all armed and in uniform. Bushell had little difficulty in locating the camp at Obies, but he and his men, now including the men at the Obies camp, bivouacked in the forest as German activity was ever increasing.

News of the forest reached the Château de Bellignies by way of a young girl named Rosa, who approached Marie de Croy with a note from Lieutenant Bushell. She explained that she and her father had found a group of English soldiers in the forest and were helping to hide them. Rosa had said that Bushell, not speaking any French, had said something about "*Bellignies*" and an "*English officer*". She also spoke of a "*mysterious spectacled lady who was enquiring about soldiers hidden in the forest*", who she and her father had thought to be a German spy and whom they had seriously considered shooting. This "*mysterious spectacled lady*" was clearly Louise Thuliez.

Louise Thuliez and Henriette Moriamé followed the directions given by Rosa and made their way to meet with Lieutenant Bushell and his depleted band. Bushell planned to stay there unless there was another alarm. The 'Girl Guides' made repeated journeys to and from the new camp, carrying food and other supplies, but Thuliez writes that she felt unable to take sole responsibility for so many lives and so consulted Captain Preston in hiding at the Château de Bellignies.

The following night Louise Thuliez took Captain Preston to the camp to meet Lieutenant Bushell. The two officers had a long discussion, after which it was decided to move the camp a little further from Obies in order to improve security, lest the villagers should let slip its location. The two returned to the château that same night and Thuliez agreed to base herself at Obies so that she might be the only visitor to the camp rather than the entire local population knowing its whereabouts. It was also agreed that at the first alarm, the men should be taken to the

Château de Bellignies. The following day, Louise Thuliez returned to Obies.

The general pattern of life at Obies was that each morning Louise Thuliez would travel into the forest with provisions for the day and then secrete herself in a small clearing outside of the camp for the remainder of the day, keeping watch for any approaching villagers. Each evening, around six o'clock, a trusted aide would bring the evening meal and then Thuliez would travel back to Obies in company with them. Thuliez had found an old charcoal stove in a woodcutter's hut, and this was used to re-heat the soup which was brought from the village each morning. The constant search for dry wood also provided the men with occupation during the cold days and helped to pass the hours.

On the fifteenth of November the evening meal did not arrive at the camp at the usual time. Finally, at about nine o'clock, Henriette Moriamé and one of the young girls from the inn at Obies arrived with the expected food. It had been impossible for them to make the journey earlier as there was increased German activity in the area, presumably searching for the fugitives. Consulting with their helpers in Obies, the girls were advised to strike camp and to make for the Château de Bellignies. Returning to speak with Lieutenant Bushell, they found him, and the men, reluctant to make a move. However, in the end the decision was made, and all signs of the camp, and anything that could incriminate the villagers, was obliterated.

LEAVING THE FOREST

The men left their forest camp at about eleven o'clock that evening, carrying their kit and whatever provisions were remaining. In order to pass through occupied villages without raising the alarm, they muffled their footsteps by wearing socks on over their boots. The fugitives travelled in two groups, the first led by Henriette Moriamé and the second by Louise Thuliez and Lieutenant Bushell. The route took them from Obies, through Bermeries and Saint-Waast-la-Vallée, and then on to Bellignies, arriving at the château at two o'clock in the morning. On the first stage of the journey torrential rain kept potential onlookers indoors, but later the rain cleared and bright moonlight forced them to take refuge until the sky clouded over again.

Once at the Château de Bellignies, Henriette Moriamé made the men comfortable in the tool-house. Louise Thuliez and Lieutenant Bushell went to the château to meet with Captain Preston, and it was decided that the two officers should spend the rest of the night together in the attic over the porter's lodge. By the morning, Preston and Bushell had made the decision that the men should give themselves up as prisoners to ensure their safety. The two girls were totally opposed to that decision. Louise Thuliez writes, "*We had already risked so much for them that we wanted to save them at any cost. After a long discussion with Captain Preston we decided to go as far as Aulnoye to see if there was not a possibility of passing the lines*".

The 'Girl Guides' were clearly devastated by the decision made in their absence and their disappointment is most clearly expressed in Louise Thuliez's own words:

> *We started out in a drenching rain, with sad hearts but stubbornly resolved to find an issue. We had forty kilometres to cover on foot, without training and with no proper walking-shoes. We found that the bridges over the Sambre were unguarded but the railway line was closely watched over since the vain attempt that the Englishmen had made to blow it up between Aulnoye and Landrecies. However we thought that a band of thirty armed men could well have overcome one or two sentries and got across.*

When we got back in the evening we were deeply disappointed. It had been decided that the men should give themselves up. In our absence the Captain had pointed out that in the face of the growing danger, it was not 'honourable' on their part to let two women go on risking their lives to save them. When we got back again we insisted that we were more than willing to go on finding food for them. But it was of no avail. Their resolve was taken on the advice of their Captain.

The girls, despite their acute disappointment with the decision, undertook to deliver the men to Monsieur Dérome, the mayor of Bavay. They were put up for the night in the Red Cross Hospital, previously the Priests' College, and the girls "*parted from them heartbroken at not having been able to save them*". The next day Monsieur Dérome handed the men over to the Germans, who clearly doubted that they had been living on forest vegetation and what they could catch. The soldiers were sent to Quesnoy and then to the prison camp at Wittenberg, where they were held until the end of the war. Despite protestations to the contrary, the Germans imposed a heavy fine on all the villages in the forest, and Monsieur Dérome was held hostage until payment was made.

Louise Thuliez makes an interesting comment on the effect Preston's decision had on Bushell and conceded the ultimate wisdom of that decision:

Lieutenant Bushell, who had not known until too late of the surrender of his men, had such a fit of despair when he heard the news that he had to have his revolver taken from him.

But we were convinced of the wisdom of Captain Preston's decision when, some days later, the snow began to fall heavily. We were forced to admit that very soon it would have been impossible to disguise our tracks on the forest paths. Had we continued, we should certainly have been taken prisoners and shot.

COMBING THE FOREST

The subsequent escape of Captain Preston and Lieutenant Bushell from the Château de Bellignies, via Edith Cavell in Brussels, to Holland was the catalyst for Louise Thuliez and Henriette Moriamé to increase their efforts to locate English and French marooned after the retreat from Charleroi and Mons. The girls realised that they needed to structure their efforts, including a relay system of 'watchers' and guides, to ensure that they had the best chance of success. Provisioning with food and clothing was, by this time, almost impossible. The country people, accustomed to raise chickens or rabbits, had any such livestock requisitioned by the Germans, and cultivation in the fields was at a standstill as so many men were serving.

Marie de Croy also comments on the increased efforts to find further fugitives in the forest and writes that the girls were assisted in the searches by Reginald de Croy and Jeanne de Belleville. Men were first taken to the Château de Bellignies for a few days' rest and then taken by Reginald de Croy to Brussels, where Edith Cavell hid them in her hospital, masquerading as invalids. She does say that Reginald de Croy had to give up conducting the men himself as he had begun attracting attention from the authorities.

The 'Girl Guides' appear to have ranged over a vast area of the forest and surrounding countryside, acting on their own and with other groups, as well as with the de Croys, based just north of the Mormal Forest. Louise Thuliez writes that, after spending such a long time in hiding, the soldiers' inaction and frustration had a most demoralising effect on them. It was difficult to reason with them and get them to wait patiently for an opportunity to escape back to their own lines. She gives, as an example, three Englishmen in hiding near Englefontaine, which was heavily garrisoned by the Germans. The girls relocated them to Ghissignies, about six kilometres away, but within a week the three had become bored and had returned to Englefontaine only to become trapped there for some months.

Rumours that an English colonel was hiding in Solesmes meant that Louise Thuliez and Henriette Moriamé needed to make that journey to Solesmes, but such a journey needed a 'pass', and so Louise Thuliez went first to Valenciennes to meet with René Delame, president of the Red Cross workers. Having got from him a written order for bandages to be collected from the Red Cross depot in Solesmes, she was then able to obtain an official 'laissez-passer' and arrived there safely. Once there she found that there were no English officers in the town, but there were many English soldiers hiding in Caudry.

Thuliez's contact in Solesmes was Mme Ladent, the wife of a French officer, who told her about German conscripted labour in the area being forced to make parts for hand-grenades. Such information would be of use to the Allies, but Mme Ladent also gave Thuliez specimens of the parts they were making. It would have been too dangerous to attempt the journey back to Saint-Waast-la-Vallée without an official 'permit to travel', so she returned to the passport office and obtained a pass on the basis that she was a Red Cross nurse having finished her period at the Valenciennes hospital, and she wanted to return home. She returned home without incident, and the hand-grenade parts were sent onward via 'diplomatic bag'.

It was during this phase of operations that the 'Girl Guides' first became aware of the escape group led by Evance Maillard at Maroilles, his wife being English by birth. Louise Thuliez and Henriette Moriamé journeyed to Maroilles, presented themselves in the name of Mme Besnard of Valenciennes, who had first told them about the Maillards, but were very aware that the entire Maillard family viewed them with suspicion. They were offered accommodation for the night and, by the following morning, were accepted as French patriots.

They then learnt of a group of twelve English soldiers who had been living underground in the marshes near Prisches for the previous six months. Louise Thuliez likened them to "*rabbits in a warren, kept alive only by the charity of some of the good people of Prisches*". In order to evacuate these men from Prisches to the Mormal Forest, it was necessary to cross the railway line which was, by then, heavily guarded by the Germans. However, the local population was allowed to cross the railway line at specified times, on specified days, in order to gather fuel. For those too old or weak to gather fuel for themselves, the Germans allowed a local farmer and some of his men to take two carts into the forest every day in order to supply the poor and needy.

Thuliez and Moriamé approached Monsieur Applincourt, the farmer, who agreed to assist in relocating the soldiers by transporting them, disguised as his woodcutters, across the railway line in his carts. Ahead of them the two girls, dressed as locals, would cross into the forest and would then wait at a pre-arranged location to take the soldiers, on foot, through the forest to its northern limit and then on to the Château de Bellignies. The number of soldiers continued to grow beyond the original twelve hiding at Prisches, and included both English and French, but finally that method of evacuation had to be terminated, as the Germans began to question the number of woodcutters entering the forest being so much greater than those returning.

Although writers heap praise upon the French civilians who gave their support and their meagre rations in support of the refugees and the organisations which helped them escape, support was not universal. Marie de Croy cites the case of the Legrand family:

> *There was also the sergeant, Robert Penniket, of the 1st Loyal North Lancashire Regiment, who with a comrade had been cut off in August, and had been hidden by the Legrand family ever since. He told us how since their arrival the legends had had to defend them from both friends and enemies. Timid inhabitants fearing reprisals were they discovered had adjured Madame Legrand to send the Englishmen away, and frequent visits from Germans had forced them to take refuge in strange places, sometimes for hours at a time behind clothes in a press, sometimes for days together in a duck-hut near the river, where old Madame Legrand brought them food by night.*

As more and more soldiers were rescued and sent on to Holland, the search for men in hiding broadened. Journeying from Bellignies to Cambrai, a distance of about thirty-five miles, meant a two day march for the 'Girl Guides', travelling only at night. The Curé of Salesches, l'Abbé Deschoedt, offered his presbytery as a resting place en route, and the two girls made use of that retreat on many occasions. Quite separately from those brought to him by the 'Girl Guides', the curé offered help to many men who presented themselves and even constructed a hiding place behind the alter of his church.

The burden on the two girls was not without its humour or, at any rate, its characters. The men in hiding were sometimes quite settled in their outlaw life. Louise Thuliez writes:

> *It was sometimes very difficult to collect men, and get them to decide on leaving their hiding-places. They had*

found good friends, and the thought of the danger they ran was not enough to make them desire to leave.

The people of Salesches still talk of a certain soldier, Tom Hanley by name, whose almost legendary foolhardiness and obstinacy made everybody wish him safely away. The people implored us to take him away before he got them all arrested with him. Easier said than done. Hanley was quite contented with his surroundings and did not, in the least, see why he should leave the country. At last with the help of the Curé of Salesches we persuaded Tom to let us guide him to the frontier.

He accompanied us one night with a rather large party of men. With his comrades he halted at Bellignies, crossed the Belgian frontier, was guided to Brussels, stayed at Miss Cavell's nursing home, allowed for Miss Cavell to arrange for his passage over the frontier, but instead of crossing into Holland, he found his way back alone to the village of Englefontaine, whence we had enticed him with such difficulty, and resumed his normal life which had already caused his protectors such anxiety. He had seen the working of our entire secret organisation and we were worried lest when he was drunk - a state in which he was more often than not - he should give us all away. We did our best on other occasions to get him to come away. But he refused and continued to live at Englefontaine until he was arrested in 1916.

However perilous the forest, the open country between it and the Château de Bellignies represented far greater risk of discovery by the Germans. In peacetime the journey on foot could be accomplished in about four hours: under occupation that same journey took six or seven hours. Although they travelled during the curfew and were unlikely to be observed by the general population, the consequence of being intercepted by German patrols was potentially catastrophic. Much time was wasted in following circuitous routes and hiding in ditches until the route was clear. In addition to wearing dark clothing, the men also blacked out their white faces and wore sandals with rope soles to minimise noise.

ESCAPE POSTPONED

A group of sixty French soldiers, hiding at a hospital in Cambrai, were being looked after by a Mlle Anne-Marie L'hotellier, described by Louise Thuliez as an "*heroic nurse*". Mlle L'hotellier, previously at the Infirmary of St Cyr, had been promoted to superintendent of the General Hospital of Cambrai just before the beginning of the war. She secretly housed Allied soldiers in the hospital while Germans came and went continuously by night and day. Secret, even, from staff and patients.

Louise Thuliez and Henriette Moriamé visited Mlle Anne-Marie L'hotellier with the intention of persuading the fugitives to let them escort them to Holland, and freedom. The superintendent was already acquainted with Edouard Thuliez, a cousin of Louise Thuliez, the Curé of St Druon in Cambrai. It was decided that the first group should "*try their chances*" with the 'Girl Guides' the following week. The two girls left for Bellignies with the intention of finding a stopping place for the men as it was a two day journey. Once they reached Bellignies they learnt that Edith Cavell had sent word that her clinique was being closely watched and that she could not accept any more men in transit for the time being. Thuliez and Moriamé immediately returned to Cambrai to postpone the men's departure.

NOBLESSE OBLIGE

THE CHATEAU DE BELLIGNIES

At the outbreak of the first world war the matriarch of the de Croy family, resident at the Château de Bellignies, was Elizabeth Hellyar-Parnell, the eighty-four-year-old grandmother of Marie, Leopold and Reginald de Croy. She was the widow of Charles Samuel Parnell but had retained the name Hellyar or Helgar, presumably from her mother's family. Her daughter, Elizabeth Mary Parnell took the West Country family into the aristocracy by marrying Prince Alfred Emanuel von Croÿ in 1875. The family disguised its German connections by adopting the name 'de Croy'.

It was Elizabeth Mary Parnell who had purchased the Château de Bellignies before the war. The château had once been in the von Croÿ family: the English grandmother had made her contribution to the Belgian nobility.

Prince Alfred Emanuel von Croÿ, born 1842 at Dülmen in Germany, was the son of Emanuel von Croÿ and Leopoldine von Croÿ, who were first cousins: he being the son of Ferdinand Victurnien Philippe von Croÿ: she being the daughter of Alfred Franz Friedrich Philipp von Croÿ. Their two fathers were brothers, sons of Auguste Philippe Louis Emanuel von Croÿ. It was through the brothers' mother, Constance Anne Louise de Croy-Solre, that the family held property at Solre-le-Château, of which Marie de Croy makes mention.

Marie, Leopold and Reginald de Croy held the title of Prince and Princess. The Belgian nobility uses the title of Duke (Duc or Hertog) for the head of each noble family, the titles Prince and Princess being adopted by other members. The term Prince or Princess does not infer blood relationship to the Royal family. By the outbreak of the war, the family resident at the Château de Bellignies was a few steps removed from the Duke but was, nevertheless, well connected with the upper echelons of France, Belgium, Holland, England and Germany.

In the days before war was declared, Princess Marie de Croy was in London, staying with her friend Ann Violet Cavendish-Bentinck and her mother, Caroline Louisa Cavendish-Bentinck (nee Burnaby). Violet was the middle daughter of three: her younger sister being Hyacinth: her elder sister being Cecilia Nina who, after the war, married Claude Bowes-Lyon, 14th Earl of Strathmore and Kinghorne. Their daughter Elizabeth became Queen to George VI, and her daughter became Queen Elizabeth II, the reigning monarch. The de Croy family were well connected.

Marie de Croy writing about 1914 says "*We had many friends in England, my father having been attached for years to the Belgian Embassy in London, where my brother Reginald had also been Secretary or Counsellor for the last ten years*". Her brother Leopold was in the Belgian Army Reserve and spent the war away from the family and the Château de Bellignies. Marie de Croy had received her nursing diploma from Paris, and this was to dictate her role during the war. The de Croy family were reunited at the very beginning of August 1914, Marie having travelled from England and Leopold from Russia, to join Reginald at the château.

Germany crossed the Belgian border, and on the 4th August King Albert addressed parliament, an address of which Marie de Croy wrote, "*From the day when the King, voicing the mind of his whole people, showed us that our duty lay in resistance to an unjust aggression, I think a burning desire to help in the cause of right possessed us all*". King Albert was, subsequently, to take command of the Belgian Army and served through the war; his wife, Queen Elisabeth, worked as an army nurse. The full text (translation) of King Albert's rallying address follows;

> *Never, since 1839, has a more solemn hour struck for Belgium: the integrity of our territory is threatened. The very force of our righteous cause, the sympathy which Belgium, proud of her free institutions and her moral victories, has always received from other nations, and the necessity of our autonomous existence in respect of the equilibrium of Europe, make us still hopeful that the dreaded emergency will not be realised. But if our hopes are betrayed, if we are forced to resist the invasion of our soil, and to defend our threatened homes, this duty, however hard it may be, will find us armed and resolved upon the greatest sacrifices.*

Even now, in readiness for any eventuality, our valiant youth is up in arms, firmly resolved, with the traditional tenacity and composure of the Belgians, to defend our threatened country. In the name of the nation, I give it a brotherly greeting. Everywhere in Flanders and Wallonia, in the towns and in the countryside, one single feeling binds all hearts together: the sense of patriotism. One single vision fills all minds: that of our independence endangered. One single duty imposes itself upon our wills: the duty of stubborn resistance.

In these solemn circumstances two virtues are indispensable: a calm but unshaken courage, and the close union of all Belgians. Both virtues have already asserted themselves, in a brilliant fashion, before the eyes of a nation full of enthusiasm. The irreproachable mobilisation of our army, the multitude of voluntary enlistments, the devotion of the civil population, the abnegation of our soldiers' families, have revealed in an unquestionable manner the reassuring courage which inspires the Belgian people.

It is the moment for action.

I have called you together, gentlemen, in order to enable the Legislative Chambers to associate themselves with the impulse of the people in one and the same sentiment of sacrifice. You will understand, gentlemen, how to take all those immediate measures which the situation requires, in respect both of the war and of public order. No one in this country will fail in his duty.

If the foreigner, in defiance of that neutrality whose demands we have always scrupulously observed, violates

> *our territory, he will find all the Belgians gathered about their sovereign, who will never betray his constitutional oath, and their Government, invested with the absolute confidence of the entire nation. I have faith in our destinies; a country which is defending itself conquers the respect of all; such a country does not perish!*

The de Croy social standing in both France and Belgium meant that access to the decision makers, most of whom were from the nobility, was much easier than for the general population, equally eager to make a contribution - a case in point being the ease with which an offer to the French Red Cross elicited a telegraphed reply from the Marquis de Vogue, accepting the Château de Bellignies as a French Red Cross hospital for officers.

ADVANCE AND RETREAT

Once the British Expeditionary Force arrived in the area, the de Croys took on their separate responsibilities: Marie de Croy to nursing, initially at the hospital in Bavay: Reginald de Croy to billeting and translating. The head of the Red Cross in the region was a Mlle de Montfort, who came from a military family, and who accommodated Sir Charles Fergusson and Lord Graham at her house in Bavay. Reginald de Croy worked closely with all three. News reached the de Croys in Bavay that a Company of the Middlesex Regiment was arriving at the Château de Bellignies, and so they motored back home to feed and provide the men with whatever comforts they could before the Company set off again, heading to Mons.

After the battle of Mons, the retreating troops again passed through Bavay and Bellignies. Some were wounded, some were simply exhausted and in want of food and drink. Most rested and then pressed on in retreat. The most seriously wounded were tended to and put to bed in the château, although treatment, in the absence of doctors, was given by Marie de Croy with help from her household staff. It was in the aftermath of Mons that Captain Preston first entered the Château de Bellignies, severely injured and with one of his men, also severely injured. With no doctor at the château, Reginald de Croy drove them to Bavay hospital, where there were British doctors.

When it was obvious that the Germans were approaching Bellignies, Reginald de Croy ran a shuttle between the château and the hospital at Bavay for those who could travel, the four most seriously injured remaining behind. Their grandmother, also, was persuaded to leave the château but returned some hours later, having found the roads south to be congested and impassable.

The first Germans to reach Bellignies were two Uhlans, who simply rode past the gates of the château without entering. These were followed by an entire German regiment, which also passed without stopping. The first German to enter the grounds of the château was a officer who simply said, "*In an hour you will receive an Army Staff which you must lodge*". The de Croys made a very quick decision to take any remaining arms from the four remaining injured and throw them down a very old and deep cistern; all other guns in the château had already been hidden in accordance with the directive which had come from the mayor.

General von Kluck, accompanied by the Duke of Schleswig-Holstein and followed by a full entourage, arrived at the château. Kluck commanded the German First Army and had inflicted serious damage to the British at Mons and at Le Cateau. The Duke displayed considerable distrust of the de Croys and of their patients, referring to the latter as 'prisoners'. According to Marie de Croy the Germans, on the orders of the Duke of Schleswig-Holstein, inflicted considerable

pain on the wounded in order to verify that their wounds and injuries were real. The Duke, accompanied by nephew and aide-de-camp, Prince Georg of Saxe-Meiningen, displayed a complete change of character in speaking to 'the noble family'. According to Marie de Croy:

> *The Duke presented his tall, young nephew politely, and, hearing my grandmother speak English, in that tongue, which he spoke perfectly, he began a conversation as if the circumstances were quite normal. According to him, King Edward had been the instigator of the war. His jealousy of his nephew, whose Empire was getting too big in comparison with that of the British, had made him form an alliance with France and Russia, the natural enemies of*

England. But it would probably be fatal to the British Empire, as her coloured troops could never be brought to fight against white troops, and would doubtless revolt against their Suzerain.

As to Belgium, he spoke despairingly of the country, and especially of its King, notwithstanding that he himself had married a granddaughter of King Leopold II. The conversation continued for some time 'aigredoux', and the Duke's temper appeared to have changed for the worse by the end of the meal. His nephew was evidently uncomfortable, but remained polite and courteous.

Despite some protestations, the de Croys sat down to dinner with thirty-two of the German officers, conversation being generally about the war and Germany's undoubted victory. While the Duke's comments were essentially aspirational, the General was much more down to earth with his assertion that the size of the two armies would ensure German victory over the British and the French. Later, after dinner, an urgent message arrived for the two officers; General Alexander von Kluck and the Duke of Schleswig-Holstein left the Château de Bellignies that same evening, bound for the Château de Rametz.

Late the following day more Germans arrived, this time General von Bauer and the Grand Duke of Mecklenburg-Strelitz, but with a smaller entourage than their predecessors. The Grand Duke was particularly friendly and considerate, visiting the wounded and giving them cigarettes and English newspapers. The family ties between England and Germany were very obvious, with him telling Marie de Croy of his English grandmother, and of his friends in England and France. After a few days, the officers left the Château de Bellignies, leaving German wounded behind in the care of the de Croys, and were replaced by General von Kühne with "*many officers and innumerable men*".

In the days that followed, more German wounded were brought to the château and treated. The English and German soldiers sat and talked amiably together, including Lieutenant Thörl, the friend that had been brought there by Prince Georg of Saxe-Meiningen on one of his return visits from General von Kluck's staff. Lieutenant Thörl appears to have been treated as a guest, rather than a patient, by the de Croys, in that he is mentioned as lunching with the 'family'.

THE BRUSSELS CONNECTION

The Comtesse Jeanne de Belleville lived at the Château Montignies-sur-Roc near Andregnies, not far from Bellignies, but across the frontier into Belgium. She was of the French nobility from her father's side and of the Belgium nobility through her mother, the Vicomtesse d'Hendecourt. With the retreat from Mons, Jeanne de Belleville, her sister Marie and their nephew Eric de Belleville began assisting English and French soldiers, overtaken by German forces and subsequently marooned behind enemy lines.

Louise Thuliez writes at some length about Jeanne de Belleville:

> *The Countess was French. She had blue eyes and curly grey hair, aquiline nose and rapid energetic step. She seemed indefatigable; everything about her breathed simplicity, goodness and spontaneity.*

Jeanne de Belleville and her nephew managed to cross the border into France and arrived at the Château de Bellignies. She told the de Croys that she and Eric intended to set out for Brussels the following day to see if there was some way in which he could leave the country in order to enlist in the French army. This was at the time that Captain Preston and Lieutenant Bushell were hidden at the château, and, included in that conversation, they were extremely anxious to hear of any possible route through Belgium to freedom.

In Brussels, Jeanne de Belleville finally met with the Abbé de Longueville, who had been assisting English and French fugitives since the battle of Mons. He agreed to take Eric de Belleville with him on one of his clandestine crossings. The Abbé also agreed that he was willing to take men sent north to him from Montignies-sur-Roc and Bellignies. Returning from Brussels, Jeanne de Belleville again visited Bellignies and reported her progress to the de Croys and the two officers.

In Brussels, Jeanne de Belleville also made the acquaintance of Herman Capiau from Wasmes, a small mining town in the region known as the 'Borinage', which lies close to the French border. Capiau had assisted the English with directions and translation from the beginning of the conflicts. As General von Kluck pressed south, Capiau organised repatriation, initially through the Mormal forest, but later, directly towards the coast at Ostend. A Belgian barrister, Albert Libiez of Wiheries-les-Dour, brought two men to Herman Capiau at Wasmes in the hope of getting them repatriated, and he, in turn, took them on to Brussels.

In Brussels, Herman Capiau met Marie Depage, who was involved with various hospitals and nursing establishments in Brussels. She was born Marie Picard, a descendant of the Belgian royalty, and married to Antoine Depage, head of the Belgian Red Cross. In 1907 Antoine Depage had founded l'École Belge d'Infirmières Diplômées in Rue de la Culture, the nursing school to which Edith Cavell was appointed as director. Marie Depage directed Herman Capiau and his charges to the school, where Edith Cavell accepted them and, after some time nursing them back to health, sent them on their way to Holland. By introducing the resistance organisations working along the Franco-Belgian border to those operating the escape routes out of Brussels, Marie Depage can be said to have been the architect of the common cause, which ended on 12th October 1915 with the death of Edith Cavell.

Antoine Depage had left Brussels for La Panne, near Le Havre in France, at the outbreak of war, and there developed a large Red Cross hospital under the auspices of Queen Elizabeth. Shortly after her meeting with Herman Capiau, Marie Depage escaped Brussels and joined her husband in La Panne. Funds were running very low; the hospital, designed to house two hundred patients, was now accommodating two thousand. Marie Depage decided to head for the United States on a two-month fund-raising mission. By the time she was ready to return to France, she had raised $100,000 and accumulated about $50,000 of supplies. Marie Depage took passage from New York to Liverpool on the Lusitania, which was torpedoed by a German U-boat and sank on the 7th May 1915. Marie Depage, along with nearly twelve-hundred others, was drowned.

It was following Herman Capiau's meeting with Edith Cavell that the number of men being guided from France, through Belgium, into Holland increased dramatically. During this period, Louise Thuliez first made the acquaintance of Philippe Baucq, an architect who was instrumental in the publication and distribution of 'underground' newspapers such as *La Libre Belgique* and the *Mot du Soldat*. It was he who first introduced Thuliez to Edith Cavell, and, as numbers increased, the Rue de la Culture became the destination of refugees from the 'feeder' groups as well as those who made their own way to Edith Cavell from all over occupied Belgium. Of course, as the route to a sanctuary in Brussels became more widely known, security became more and more compromised and put Edith Cavell and the entire network in danger.

Eventually the pressure on Edith Cavell intensified and she asked Jeanne de Belleville to spread the word amongst the various groups that she could not accept any more refugees for the time being. Philippe Baucq had a well organised network in place and agreed to take the pressure off Edith Cavell.

REGINALD DE CROY

Despite the German occupation of Belgium and northern France, movement across the frontier, if not easy, seems not to have been too difficult for Reginald de Croy. Even before the battle of Mons, he managed to cross the frontier and make his way to Beveren-Waes, near Antwerp, to find his brother Leopold who was with the First Guides regiment, still in training.

After the fall of Maubeuge, Prince Reginald de Croy and Baron Louis de la Grange of Sebourg walked to the town and visited the hospital, from where they returned to report that the Germans had collected a great amount of guns and ammunition, which was ready to be transported to the front line. They also reported that the entire area was filled with the wounded, and they were able to arrange transport for many to be transferred to Bavay.

In early October, Reginald de Croy left for Brussels in order to obtain basic foodstuffs from the American Committee, which he did, and then, having obtained a pass from the Germans, left for Holland, using the excuse of having to procure funds. The banks in occupied territory were generally closed, but money was still required for daily living but also to pay the innumerable fines imposed by the Germans on the local population. Having reached Holland, he sailed to England with Prince Albert de Ligne and then on to Havre, where the Belgian Government was established. On his return journey, Reginald de Croy spent twenty-four hours in London with Captain Preston's family, finally arriving in Bellignies towards the end of November.

Some time later, Reginald de Croy obtained a second pass for Holland, again on the pretence of procuring funds. He again travelled to Havre and on the way back through London called in at the War Office. Before boarding the boat for Flushing, he picked up an English newspaper which carried a paragraph detailing the escape of twelve soldiers, who, having been hidden in a château in northern France, then escaped via Belgium. This was a group that had been hidden at the Château de Bellignies and had made their escape via the Rue de la Culture; coincidently Reginald de Croy had met one of the escaped officers at the War Office before he left London. A telephone call was sufficient to alert the censor about further articles, but, as Marie de Croy writes:

> *The men themselves frequently forgot that although they were in safety once they got to Holland, we were left behind in the power of the enemy, and several wrote postcards of thanks to Miss cavell and others who had lodged them.*

As the Germans closed in on the escape organisations, and arrests began to be made, Reginald de Croy travelled again to Brussels. Once there, he spent time visiting several safe houses and learnt of even more arrests. He returned to Bellignies to hear that Herman Capiau had also been arrested. Returning to Brussels again, he quickly had to go into hiding, and it was some time before he could get across the border into Holland, this time without a pass.

Reginald de Croy made his escape with the aid of Henri Beyns, and, having travelled by tram as far as Vilvorde, they then continued on foot and got across the River Dyle. At this stage they were joined by another refugee, Monsieur van Maldeghem, who was also trying to get to Holland. They passed through the Mérodes' woods and on to Baelen via the Abbey of Tongerloo. Eventually they swam the canal and walked the last seven kilometres to the border, reaching safety at daybreak.

THE NET CLOSES

The Germans began to target the members of the escape organisations in a more overt manner than before. The Château de Bellignies was thoroughly searched by a group of soldiers, numbering over forty men, and lasting a number of hours. While this was going on, sixteen English soldiers were hidden in the tower, and it was to their great relief when they were finally able to leave their confined retreat.

Marie de Croy, visiting Edith Cavell in Brussels, was told that Cavell thought herself to be under surveillance. Her concern must have been serious, as she told her visitor that she had taken the precaution of burning all her records, having had a German search party visit her the previous day. Both women agreed that they should cease their activities forthwith. On reflection, however, they agreed that they would need to continue in some capacity, as Louise Thuliez and Henriette Moriamé had men already in the pipeline, but they would limit their activity to communications rather than to actually guiding men.

On her return to the Château de Bellignies news came that Philippe Baucq, Edith Cavell and Louise Thuliez had all been arrested in Brussels. Some time later Jeanne de Belleville was taken away by the Germans, but her mother and sister were obviously not implicated and remained at the Château Montignies-sur-Roc.

An entrapment of Marie de Croy was attempted by a German, Otto Meyer, who pretended to be an escaped British prisoner who had been in hiding in Brussels. He said that he had heard from a priest that the de Croys could help him get back to rejoin his regiment. Her advice to him was to give himself up to the authorities as he was putting himself and others in danger. A day or two later the château was again visited by German troops, this time looking for Reginald de Croy, but they were led, incorrectly, to believe that he was at their other property at Solre-le-Château, which gave him a little more leeway in his flight to Holland. The Germans came back a few days later when they concentrated on searching for papers and files in Reginald de Croy's study. Again, the Germans left the château but this time put up road blocks so that nobody could get in or out of Bellignies.

The Germans who came to arrest Marie de Croy arrived by car in the very early morning. They were Lieutenant Pinkhoff and Lieutenant Bergan and required her to travel with them by rail to Brussels, ostensively as a witness to an incident concerning a French aeroplane landing in the area. During the journey to Brussels, Marie de Croy was constantly questioned by the two Germans, who told her that others arrested had made full statements implicating her in all the activities and, specifically, that Edith Cavell had admitted to having received funds from her to pay for guides and other expenses. From the train she was driven to Saint-Gilles prison, where she and Jeanne-de-Belleville were questioned together. Later they were taken to separate cells and interrogated separately.

PHILIPPE BAUCQ

When Louise Thuliez visited Brussels she stayed at a small hotel owned by one of her helpers near the Gare du Midi. As it had been decided that no more refugees were to be sent to Edith Cavell for the time being, she felt it necessary to discuss the details of how Philippe Baucq was to begin receiving such men. Having been offered a room for the night at his home, Thuliez returned to her hotel, collected her bag and spent some time attending to other matters before arriving at Baucq's house at about a quarter to eleven in the evening as the entire family was engaged in folding copies of the *Libre Belgique*.

Philippe Baucq opened the front door to let his dog out for a short run before the family retired for the night. As he did so, Germans rushed through the open door and up the stairs to where Louise Thuliez was being shown to her room by Mme Baucq. They had been watching the house and were looking for Thuliez, and she gave her latest alias, Mme Lejeune, but could not give them an address. The house was thoroughly searched before Louise Thuliez and Philippe Baucq were taken, on the orders of Inspector Pinkhoff, to the police station in Rue de la Loi and then to Saint Gilles Prison.

EDITH CAVELL

On the 6th of August 1915 the nurses at the clinique in Rue de la Culture were very much occupied with moving to their new premises on the corner of Rue de Bruxelles and Rue de l'École. Three Germans, dressed in civilian clothes, entered the building in Rue de la Culture. Jacqueline van Til describes the men:

> *The expression on their faces was exultingly gleeful. They laughed and talked together in German, pointing the while at Sister Wilkins and Mania. I inferred from this that we were now fallen into the merciless hands of the Boches, who were gloating over the fact that we had finally been caught in their net. They commanded us not to move, and*

> *pointing their revolvers at our heads, they roughly pushed us into a corner of the room. We now fully realised that we were prisoners.*

Edith Cavell was arrested and put into one car, Sister Wilkins into another. Protesting nurses were threatened with guns, and the two cars left at about four o'clock in the afternoon, but Sister Wilkins returned to Rue de la Culture about nine o'clock that same evening. The nurses were allowed to move freely within the clinic but were accompanied by a German soldier whenever they went outside. Despite many requests, they were unable to get any news of Edith Cavell except that there was a request for a change of clothes, which Sister Wilkins delivered, but she was not allowed to see her. The Germans continued to have an overt presence at both clinics for some time.

GEORGES GASTON QUIEN

FIRST IMPRESSIONS

Dated 17th October 1918, a file copy of a Security Services report, KV 2/844 (originally PF37346), held by the National Archives in Kew, makes reference to resistance activities in Belgium and northern France, and identifies Georges Gaston Quien, also known as Luc/ Pierreson or as Pierre Pierron. Quien was born on the 28th May 1879 at Saint Sulpice-Ham, Somme, in that part of France called Picardy, to Joseph Alfred Quien and his wife Marie Célestine Alexandrine Quien, née Dive. Quien had been living with his father in the Boulevard de Grenelle, Paris, having been divorced from his wife Eugénie Desjardin before the war; she, presently, living at 24 Rue Daniel Stern. Quien was said to be working at the La Société des Moteurs Salmson in the Avenue des Moulineaux, Seine.

The report said that it was Quien who approached the British in the last weeks of the war, offering valuable information on the Edith Cavell organisation and on enemy agents in Switzerland. Records showed that Quien had previously been denounced by a certain Pierre Enel as having acted as a local spy for the Germans, and to have been addressed as *"my dear friend"* by Max Levy, a notorious enemy agent in Brussels. Quien was interviewed at Annemasse, in July, having already been arrested by the French Police. It was noted that he was treated very leniently by the Germans on each occasion that he had been arrested by them in the past.

Towards the end of hostilities some members of the Cavell group were repatriated to Rouen, where they were interviewed by British Intelligence and made allegations about Quien. Aubertine Houet (the married sister of Louise Thuliez), Jeanne Cleve, Betty Van Baer (the married daughter of Evance Maillard): all were convinced that Quien had been working for the Germans. The interviewees all claimed that Leopold de Croy would also be able to give information concerning Quien, but he was only able to pass on his brother Reginald's suspicions.

Quien, when interviewed, claimed that he was sent to the Sennelager internment camp in Germany and from there to Interlaken in Switzerland. It was found later that Quien had also been at Holzminden prisoner of war camp between his times in Sennelager and Interlaken. Pierre Enel was also at Sennelager (see his comments above). Also at Interlaken, was Julien Launais, who claimed that Quien was a local spy and one who enjoyed an "*abnormal amount of liberty*".

Julien Launais had come into contact with Quien at both Holzminden and Interlaken and said that, at Holzminden, Quien had *"daily conversations with the Commandant of the camp, one Captain Witkopl, and was frequently in the company of two Feldwebels (NCOs) named Albin and Lan"*. According to Julien Launais it was well known to all the interred that Quien and an un-named Belgian were the denunciators of the camp. Quien was definitely not unwell and his being billeted in the infirmary was to afford him more favourable treatment. *"Quien enjoyed very great liberty, being allowed frequently to go into town, and unguarded"*.

The assessment of Quien in the report is that his statements were certainly not the whole truth and that he had been paid by Germany to act as a double-agent. The assessment of Quien was, that under interrogation he made a "*distinctly bad impression*" and that he had been on "*extremely intimate terms with the enemy agents he [now] denounces*".

Pierre Enel confirmed the unusual relationship that Quien had with the Germans. It seems that a few days before Quien's arrival at Sennelager the Germans had emptied and refurnished a small room in one of the barracks.

> *Quien had been given this room, and was exempted from all work in the camp. He was well treated by the camp officials, he spent most of his time in or near the canteen, and took great pains to make friends with the other prisoners.*

Towards the end of his stay in Sennelager, Pierre Enel said that Quien was transferred to the camp hospital, despite him showing no sign of ill health, and later was reported as being sent to Switzerland as an incurable invalid, although he was said to have been later seen in Berne.

Betty Van Baer, the married daughter of Evance Maillard, who was active in the Mormal Forest, also confirmed Quien's strange relationship with the Germans while a civilian prisoner at Landrecies. Again *"he enjoyed an extraordinary measure of liberty, and was given quite different treatment to other civilian prisoners in there"*. She said that Quien was generally mistrusted and was thought to be a possible German agent, so much so that her father refused to put him in direct contact with the Cavell organisation but simply sent him through to Mons. It was there that he made contact with Louise Thuliez, who then took him through to Brussels.

INTERROGATION

The following dossier was sent to Major Menzies at GHQ Paris, dated 28th June 1918, and signed by a Captain S.P. Best. In his covering note, Captain Best says that during his interrogation of Quien, he had avoided doing anything to arouse Quien's suspicions, but that intelligence matters of this kind were outside of his experience.

> *According to QUIEN'S <u>own account</u> the main points in his career during the war are as follows:-*
>
> *Having avoided registration he was arrested by the Germans as a suspect in March 1915 when attempting to effect his escape from St. QUENTIN to BRUSSELS.*
>
> *Was sent as prisoner to LANDRECIES and was employed in felling timber in FORET DE MORMAL.*
>
> *While there got in touch with organisation engaged in evacuation of men of military age and of British soldiers hidden in the FORET DE MORMAL to BRUSSELS and thence to Holland.*
>
> *On 29th May 1915 with 40 other men of which 20 were British soldiers he was evacuated from Landrecies by an agent named by MAILLARD EVANCE who was working under the PRINCE DE CROY at BELLIGNIES and under MISS CAVELL at BRUSSELS.*
>
> *He reached BRUSSELS on 4th June 1915 and states that he was then taken into the services of the CAVELL organisation working for it until 18th June when he was sent to Holland on a mission to the PRINCE ALBERT DE LIGNE at the HAGUE.*
>
> *He arrived at the Hague on 20th June 1915 and saw the PRINCE DE LIGNE and also LT. COLONEL DESPREY*

French military attaché to whom he delivered messages from Miss Cavell and from the Prince de Croy.

He was ordered by Lt. Colonel Desprey to return to Brussels and to place himself at the disposition of Miss Cavell.

He left Holland on 22nd June 1915 and owing to difficulties experienced while crossing the frontier did not succeed in reaching BRUSSELS till 29th July 1915.

He states that he reported to Miss CAVELL on 1st August 1915 but that by 5th August 1915 all the members of her organisation had been arrested.

Informant himself escaped arrest and, according to his own account, under the false name of PIERRON, GASTON in which his identity papers were made out, carried on with the work of evacuating men of military age into Holland and also furnished reports to some S.S. organisations.

On 19th November 1915 Informant was himself arrested having been implicated in the MISS CAVELL affair by BODAERT [actually Bodart] who under cross examination had stated that he [Quien] was a French agent.

QUIEN was imprisoned at ST GILLES and from December 1915 to 23rd July 1916 was kept in solitary confinement on a diet of bread and water. During this period he was confronted with a large number of people, was subjected to interrogation on the part of German secret police officials and appeared before 5 courts marshal.

On 23rd July 1916 informant was sent as a civilian prisoner to SENNELAGER where he states he was at once sent to the Lazarett [or sick bay] remaining there during the whole time of his internment at the camp. He states that he was suffering from Gastro-enteritis and General debility and was never able to leave his bed.

On the 1st December 1916 he left SENNELAGER for internment in SWITZERLAND being sent to INTERLAKEN where he was lodged at the HOTEL LE SOLEIL

Here Captain Best notes an entry in the Evian Diary No. 329 page 2369 last paragraph:

SENNELAGER

QUIEN:- thought to be a French subject, age about 46. Very tall and thin; said that he had come from ST. QUENTIN. Managed to get a special room for himself and without being appointed to any special post exempted from all work. He arrived in SENNELAGER in March 1916 and is now thought to be at the French Legation at BERNE.

Should be strictly watched. He is said to have been addressed as 'mon cher ami' by a German Secret Police official in Belgium by name of LEVY, MAX when on visit to SENNELAGER.

The dossier continues:

The above description absolutely fits QUIEN who is about 6 ft 2 inches in height and remarkably thin. Neither the date of his arrival at Sennelager or the account of his movements there tally with his own account. He did however under interrogation mention a German S.S. agent of the name LEVY whom he met at BRUSSELS.

> *QUIEN interrogated as to his life at SENNELAGER insisted that he was in hospital the whole time and never left his bed.*
>
> *QUIEN remained at the HOTEL LE SOLEIL at INTERLAKEN during the whole period of his stay in SWITZERLAND.*
>
> *He states that he was appointed Quartermaster to the HOTEL by the CHEF DE SECTEUR, ADJUDANT DE GOUY and then enjoyed greater liberty than others interned who were only allowed out of their quarters at certain times of the day.*
>
> *He states that at INTERLAKEN he got into touch with a certain Baron ERICH DE DITTEMAR and with a German S.S. organisation controlled by him.*

The dossier refers, at this point, to written reports by Quien, detailing his movements in Belgium and the details learnt by him as to the activities of the above S.S. organisation. These reports are not included in the archives. The dossier continues:

> *It should be noted that QUIEN under interrogation gives these written reports almost word for word. In this he displays an astonishingly good memory for names, dates [and] places which memory however fails him completely when he is asked to furnish any complimentary details.*
>
> *During the whole of his stay at INTERLAKEN, QUIEN was apparently in constant association with de DITTEMAR and with the latter's friends. He appears to have gone on excursions with them and to have enjoyed an extraordinary measure of liberty. This strikes me as curious as on another occasion he spoke to us about the restrictions placed on the movements of interred in*

Switzerland and also gave a description of the state of his health which would lead me to believe that he would have been unable to carry out the counter-espionage work he reports.

On 2nd January 1918 his health was so bad that he was repatriated from Switzerland as incurable. He passed through ANNEMASSE on 2nd January 1918 but states that he was never interrogated there but was passed straight to his depot at LORIENT (45e D'INFANTERIE)

Here Captain Best notes another entry in the Evian Diary:

QUIEN, GASTON GEORGES

Arrêté la Police Francaise 30th August 1917 a ANNEMASSE

The dossier continues:

Arrived at his depot he informed the authorities that he had important information to give and he was accordingly sent to the B.C.R XI e Regim at NANTES.

He produces a movement order headed

SERVICE DE LA CIRCULATION

1 RUE D'ARGENTRE NANTES

and signed by MATTEY for ETAT MAJOR XI e REGION

which states that he was to appear there for interrogation on 29th January 1918

QUIEN states that he communicated all the information contained in the 2 attached reports [not included] and that he was then sent for further interrogation to the Ministre de la Guerre at Paris.

In support of this statement he produces an AVIS DE MUTATION dated 2nd February 1918 ordering him to proceed to Paris. Ministre de la Guerre he was subjected to further interrogation by a Captain in the French Intelligence Service by whom he was told that his information was interesting, and that he would be rewarded.

He was given 2 months leave in Paris where he has remained to the present date having been under medical treatment at various military hospitals.

Captain Best sums up as follows:

The impression made by QUIEN on Inspector Ide and myself on the three occasions when he has been seen by us is not favourable.

Under cross examination his story lacks a certain air of reality and his evident inability to amplify the account given in his written statement was most striking.

It should also be noted that various statements contained in his report as to conditions of registration in Belgium in 1914 and 1915 are chronologically wrong, whilst the details he is able to give as to the identity and personality of people with whom he is supposed to have worked are so vague that it is hard to believe that he can ever have met them.

He displays great anxiety to obtain a hearing and seems too anxious to establish his bona fides by means of documentary evidence whilst he is unable to give facts unless about himself and about his work not contained in his report.

It would appear to me well worth while to make further enquiries about QUIEN and if possible to have him confronted by the informant who gave information about him contained in EVIAN Report No. 329.

QUIEN was not allowed to suspect the existence of this report or that we know anything further about him than what he has told us himself, we have merely thanked him for his efforts and told him that he shall hear from us again.

COURT MARSHAL

Georges Gaston Quien was put on trial before a French court-marshal, held in Paris on 25th August 1919, which was reported in Britain by *The Daily Telegraph*, under the headline:

> THE BETRAYER OF NURSE CAVELL: SPY'S BAD RECORD: STORY OF TREACHERY: *Tall, thin and somewhat haggard, the man who is alleged to have betrayed Edith Cavell today faced his judges in Paris. Georges Quien, on account of his height, bears the nickname of 'Double Metre'. The accusation against him is a terrible one. He is alleged to have denounced, not only the heroic British nurse who did so much for the French, British and Belgians over whom had passed the swift German flood, but also many other victims of his treachery are mentioned in the charge against him. Presiding over the bench of the military judges was Lieut-Colonel Camut, solemn and erect, listening to the scathing report which has been drawn up against Quien. On the Government bench was no longer, as at previous military trials, the wild*

bearded Captain Mornet. The prosecution is being conducted by Lieutenant Wagner.

When Quien appeared in the dock today in his faded military uniform, pale, his little lively eyes glancing uneasily from side to side, there was the usual interrogatory of identity: "Your profession?" – "Business man": "Your previous domicile?" – "Saint Quentin". He rapped out these replies briskly, without a trace of emotion, but as the story was unfolded his pallor disappeared, and his bony countenance was crimsoned with shame. One surprise reserved by the defence, which was being conducted by Maître Henri Darmont, is to demand that, in conformity with Articles 228 and 230 of the Treaty of Versailles no judgement shall be pronounced until Von Bissing and other Germans, dead or alive, shall have been joined in the proceedings. In case this demand is rejected, an alternative is proposed that further inquiry shall be pursued as to the responsibility of the German authorities.

The articles 228 and 230 of the Treaty of Versailles state that The German Government recognises the right of the Allied and Associated Powers to bring before military tribunals persons accused of having committed acts in violation of the laws and customs of war. Such persons shall, if found guilty, be sentenced to punishments laid down by law. This provision will apply notwithstanding any proceedings or prosecution before a tribunal in Germany or in the territory of her allies. The German Government shall hand over to the Allied and Associated Powers, or to such one of them as shall so request, all persons accused of having committed an act in violation of the laws and customs of war, who are specified either by name or by the rank, office or employment which they held under the German authorities. The German Government undertakes to furnish all documents and information of every kind, the production of which may be considered necessary to ensure the full knowledge of the incriminating acts, the discovery of offenders and the just appreciation of responsibility.

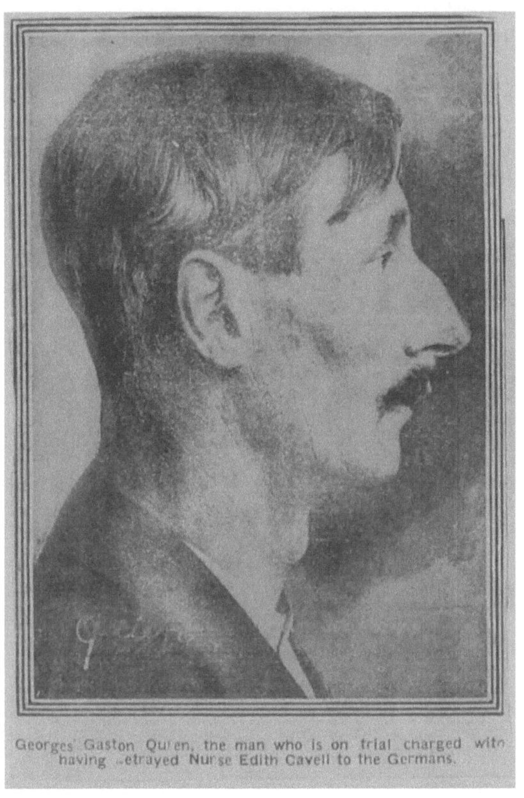

Georges Gaston Quien, the man who is on trial charged with having betrayed Nurse Edith Cavell to the Germans.

A CROWDED COURT: The affair, chiefly because of its connection with the death of the heroic Miss Cavell. Attracted great interest, and even in these dog days a considerable audience crowded the gloomy court. There must be at least twelve sittings. Most of the witnesses, who number eighty, are victims of Quien. As to the personality of the accused, it is impossible to discover the smallest ground of sympathy for him. He is an adventurer, without scruple of any kind; his reputation is that of a drunkard and a lazy débauché. His wife, after an experience of his cruelty, was forced to seek a divorce. A native of the Aisne, 40 years of age, he has been four times convicted in France, twice for robbery, once for swindling, and once for an affair of discipline in the army. When the Germans came to Saint Quentin in 1914, he was in prison. Taken to Landrecies as a civil prisoner, he illegally exercised the profession of doctor under the name of Caduret. He also described himself as a French officer, and again as an advocate. He even pretended to be attached to the Embassy. He wormed his way into the confidence of those devoted persons who had organised a system of repatriating Allied soldiers caught by the enemy in Belgium and the Northern provinces of France. These soldiers were smuggled out of the invaded regions by way of Holland. There were many men who had managed to hide themselves in the Forest of Mormal [written here as Marolle]. It is clear that he managed to put himself in good relations with the Prince de Croy and with Miss Cavell. He himself went to Holland, but returned to Brussels, where he had a double-faced existence, frequenting at the same time patriotic Belgian circles and the offices of the German police. His whole career seems to be more than suspect, and although he may not be the sole author of the four condemnations to death which are attributed to him, he is regarded as being principally responsible for the execution of Nurse Cavell.

It was at Brussels, Rue de la Culture, that Miss Cavell directed a school of nursing, in which she gave shelter to the fugitives. Most of them were sent to her from the Château *of Bellignies. That was the principal centre of the various secret organisations which were formed to facilitate the passage into Holland. It was directed by*

Prince Reginald de Croy and his sister, Princess Marie de Croy. The fugitives there received all the necessary money and papers, and the home of Miss Cavell was one of the final stages in their pilgrimage.

It was the generous imprudence of a young girl employed on a farm at Landrecies which acquainted Quien with the secret of the association of which the Prince de Croy was the head. He seems to have had intimate relations with the young woman, promised to marry her, borrowed 50f, and was taken by her to the château. The Prince furnished him with several hundred francs. According to the report of Captain Grebaut, he then came into contact with another member of the daring association, Mlle. Thuliez, who gave him lunch, and he went on to Mons, where the engineer Cappiau, also in the secret, provided him with the essential identity certificates. Under the protection of Mlle. Thuliez he reached Brussels, and lodged in the house of Miss Cavell, in company with another refugee – a real refugee – named Motte, of Roubaix. He was to have left in two or three days, but he managed to delay his departure. He frequented the cafés where he drank too much, and he flirted with the servants of the Cavell Institute. Miss Cavell at last took him herself, in company with sixteen other fugitives, to Turnhout, and finally, at the end of June 1915, Quien arrived at The Hague.

The reference to the 'real refugee', Motte, is at odds with Jacqueline Van Til's account of Mr. X. It appears that Motte was Quien's companion on arrival in Brussels, that he also behaved very suspiciously and that the guide, Victor Gilles, thought that caution should be exercised in dealings with him.

IN THE GERMAN TOILS: Why did he come back to Belgium? He pretends that it was to serve the Allies. He went to see the French Military Attaché at the Hague, Colonel Desprez, and offered himself as an agent of counter-espionage. Here he obtained 500 francs and was soon once more in Belgium. His own story is that he was arrested by the Germans, sent to Antwerp, and condemned to six weeks' imprisonment for travelling without a passport. It is true that he was arrested. Was that arrest a mere comedy? The theory of the prosecution is that this measure was only taken to supply him with good credentials for his work of spying for the Germans. It is certainly strange that, without further inquiry, the Germans authorised him to return to Brussels.

At the end of July Miss Cavell again saw him, and the next day he lunched with Madame Bodard. With the architect Baucq, one of the most active members of the association of the Prince de Croy, he discussed the best routes to follow to gain the frontier. Why was he accepted without suspicion? Why did the association not doubt the story of his mysterious return? These are the questions which the trial will elucidate. At any rate, three days later the denouement of the drama was reached. The Germans made wholesale arrests.

On July 31 Baucq was arrested. The Germans had seized the man who knew all the roads out of Belgium, and who, a few days before, had revealed his knowledge to Quien. At the same time Madame Bodard, with whom he had lunched, was imprisoned. Mlle. Thuliez, whom had personally conducted him to Miss Cavell, was also in custody. The apprehension of Miss Cavell was not long delayed. She and the Countess de Belleville and the Princess Marie de Croy were thrown into prison.

The trial is known, as well as the unavailing efforts of the American Ambassador to save the devoted woman, and the remorseless ferocity of the German judges, the German governor, and the German executioners. Quien, who was, if he were innocent of the betrayal, so deeply implicated from the German point of view, was left at liberty. He remained safe while Miss Cavell and the architect Baucq were murdered. The King of Spain intervened successfully in the case of the Countess de Belleville and Mlle. Thuliez, who had also received the death sentence. They were reprieved, but had the sentence commuted to one of hard labour for life. The engineer Cappiau and Madame Bodard were condemned to fifteen years imprisonment. Princess Marie de Croy escaped with the comparatively light sentence of five years. The tragedy of the death of his benefactors did not prevent Quien, according to the prosecution, from continuing.

If the denunciation of Miss Cavell and her companions is the crime which has most struck the public imagination, there are, nevertheless, other crimes no less abominable which are laid at the door of Quien. He is alleged to have led to the conviction of a good priest the Abbé Bosteels, who also occupied himself with helping his unfortunate countrymen to get to Holland. He caused the arrest of an hotel keeper with whom he lodged. The laws of hospitality did not exist for him. A Belgian police agent, perhaps rather foolishly, made certain confidences to him. They were passed on. The arrest of Madame Adam and of her three aunts is attributed to him. A man named Houtard, patriotic but imprudent, showed him a Mauser rifle hidden in his wardrobe. The imprudent patriot was prosecuted. An association which was analogous to that of Miss Cavell was broken up, and Freyling, Mademoiselle Henry, and their companion were condemned. This last case seems to have caused his own imprisonment, whether in order to save appearances or not remains to be seen. At any rate, the reporter to the court does not hesitate to say that during the three months that he was in the prison of Saint Gilles at Brussels the other prisoners discovered that he was a mere spy, the 'mouton' to use the French expression, of the German police chief, Pinkhoff.

That seems to have brought his services in Belgium to an end. He went to Switzerland. How did he manage to get there without the compliance of the German authorities? He was said to be suffering from gastric trouble, and was thus passed into the neutral country. Here it is alleged that he engaged himself in the French counter-espionage service in order to deliver up the secrets which came into his possession to the Germans. When at last he came to France, in August 1917, he was arrested for theft, proceeding in connection with which had begun before the war. After his liberation he is believed to have been guilty of swindling, crimes for which he will now have to answer, in addition to the greater crime of treason.

The Daily Telegraph also published a Reuters report which identified the young Landrecies girl, who introduced Quien to the Prince and Princess de Croy, as Jeanne Balligan. It was through one of her friends that Quien was able to pass through the Château of Bellignies and onto Mons and Brussels with sufficiently established credentials. The

Reuters report also identified a Monsieur Motte as his travelling companion from Bellignies, via Mons, to Brussels.

Over the following days the trial continued to be reported in the British newspapers. Again the fullest accounts contained in the files of the security services are from *The Daily Telegraph*. Their correspondent continued to be extremely sceptical as to Quien's evidence and explanations. When asked why he had stayed so long in Brussels with Edith Cavell, rather than follow her advice to travel quickly on through to Holland, he explained that he had an 'ingrowing toenail': asked about the coincidence of Edith Cavell's arrest shortly upon his return to Brussels, he put it down to nothing more than coincidence. The newspaper refers to the "*singular glitter of his shifting eyes, his appreciation of the character of the network of evidence woven around him*".

The president of the court named a number of people with whom Quien had come in contact and who had then been subject to arrest and interrogation by the Germans, particularly mentioning the Abbé Bosteels and Madame Vandamme. The president of the court asked Quien if he remembered Monsieur Freyling. Quien exclaimed that "*Freyling is dead – I don't know Freyling*". "*We will ask Monsieur Freyling if he knows you,*" replied the president.

Quien was questioned at length about the fact that, sooner or later, nearly all the people connected with Edith Cavell and her organisation were arrested by the Germans and either shot or sentenced to long terms of imprisonment. The newspapers reported that Quien's replies were "*either that he knew nothing of the circumstances, or that he was unable to say anything on the point as he suffered from loss of memory*".

The Daily Telegraph provided further reports, under the headline:

FRENCH SPY TRIAL: QUIEN EXAMINED: *Under the fire of cross-examination Quien stammered out lame explanations on his doings in Belgium just before the arrest of Nurse Cavell. He has lost that quickness of response which marked his earlier replies. He continues to pretend that he returned to Brussels after being helped across the frontier into Holland by Miss Cavell and those associated with her on the express orders of the French Military Attaché, and denies that he had anything to do*

GASTON QUIEN
qui dénonça miss Cavell

with the events which followed his return. The most embarrassing point for him hitherto has been the incident of the packet which was given into his custody by Madame

Bodard. Road-maps from the packet undoubtedly fell into the hands of the Germans. He was visibly disconcerted when pressed by the President of the Court-Martial about this significant matter. The attitude of the president, Colonel Camus, is unsparing for the accused. "Not only did the maps of Madame Bodard reach the Germans", he said "but when the Abbé Bosteels gave you a document he was immediately arrested".

Quien is sometimes very prolix. At the beginning he was almost glib in his explanations of how all these persons whom he frequented were imprisoned or shot by the Germans. But now he falters more frequently. When a question which is too difficult is put to him, he hesitates and then freely answers, "You know it was because of a mental trouble which produces forgetfulness that I was put in the Auxiliary Army". "How do you account for it," pursued the President, "that in the concentration camp of Sennelager you were seen to shake hands with the German police spy Pinkhoff?" "That," replied Quien, "was because he was in civilian attire, and I mistook him for a compatriot". "That does not explain why you should call Pinkhoff my dear friend," returned the President.

Indeed, Quien's relations with German police officers are altogether highly compromising. When he was ill later in Switzerland he made the acquaintance of a spy named Dittmar [otherwise referred to as Dittemar]. "You were not only friendly, but led a joyous life with him". It should be noted, however, that the French counter-espionage service was already on the track of Dittmar, and laid a trap for him which Dittmar escaped. The interrogation left for the moment the incidents which concern the death of Miss

Cavell and dealt with some of the many other arrests which are attributed to him.

DISGRACEFUL EPISODE: The character of Quien was shown in an odious light when he was questioned to-day about the theft of £10 from the mother of one of his companions during his stay at the Sennelager in Germany. When he arrived in France in August, 1917, he made himself known to a Madame Manhes, giving her news of her son. He thus obtained the £10 from Madame Manhes in order to bury his mother. Lieutenant Wagner, who is prosecuting, put pointed questions to him about this disgraceful episode. Quien declared that he had heard one of his comrades say at the Gare du Nord, in Paris, that his mother was dead, and when he told Madame Manhes of this she freely offered the money. He accepted it and went to his home.

Wagner: What story did you tell her on your return? Quien: I regret to say that I did tell her that I had buried my mother.

It is hardly necessary to say that the mother of Quien is still alive. One crime more or less hardly counts, and, after all, what is this in comparison with the other charges which rest upon him? He seems content to admit the smaller offences to give himself an air of frankness, but with regard to the graver accusations his denials are emphatic. He had nothing to do, he protested, with the arrest of Madame Vandamme. It was not he who told the German police of the Mauser rifle which was found in the cupboard of Houtard. Nor did he denounce Madame Adam, he only said one day to the police agent Pinkhoff that he did not know if Madame Adam had, like so many more, "the hysteria of patriotism". As for Freyling, the chief of a similar organisation to that of Miss Cavell, who was also indicated to the Germans, he did not even know him. The statement of Freyling was read out to him. Quien was astonished, and exclaimed, "But he is dead".

Among the names of the witnesses cited is that of Freyling. The story of Freyling is held by the prosecution to be a clear proof of Quien's guilt, for when Freyling was put upon his trial Quien stood in the dock with him, and while Freyling was condemned to death Quien was sentenced to three months' imprisonment. The theory is that his trial was mere make-belief and that this light condemnation was simply to throw dust in the eyes of those whom he might afterwards betray.

The witnesses began to file before the Court. The first this afternoon was a young soldier named Wallace. He was employed with Quien as a cook for the civilian prisoners at Landrecies, whence, it will be remembered, Quien departed with the aid of the Prince and Princess de Croy for Brussels, where he came into contact for the first time with Miss Cavell. His evidence was as to the kind of life Quien then led. Quien was known as Doctor Perduret, and also under the name of Pierson. The nickname of 'Double Metre', on account of his height, was given to him there. The testimony served to show that Quien was often allowed out, and sometimes was absent for the whole day. Quien grew very indignant at the suggestion that he enjoyed the favour of the German authorities.

Another witness was Louis Mercier, who kept a hotel and restaurant at Saint Quentin. He fled before the German invasion. Quien and a girl with whom he was associated at that time sacked his restaurant. In this pillaging Quien employed violence. A servant who intervened was struck, and was so terrified that she became mad. The witness also accused Quien of stealing a motor-car. The whole history of Quien during his wanderings in the course of the war is full of such episodes.

The next report on the Court Marshal is taken from *The Morning Post* under the headline 'Trial of Quien – Miss Cavell's Colleagues in Witness Box – Dramatic Episodes'

The Court-marshal of Quien, now popularly nicknamed 'Double metre' owing to his great height – about six feet five inches – has its dramatic moments. Many witnesses have been heard, including the chief of a refugee organisation, all of whom are convinced that it was through Quien that they suffered the horrors of German imprisonment. There was a moment when the Court was hushed to absolute silence as the witness pointed an accusing finger at Quien, declaring: "That is the man who is responsible".

There was a profound sensation again during the evidence of Mme. Adam, who was herself imprisoned, she is convinced, as the result of betrayal by Quien, and declared that one of her aunts died as the result of her imprisonment, which was brought about by Quien. Council for the defence was attempting to shake her evidence, and challenged her with the question: "Would you, Madame, on the evidence you have laid before the Court, dare to condemn this man to death?"

"No," was the reply; and council exulted, but she turned on him with the remark: "It is not my place, Monsieur, to ask for the life of a man. I am seeking no man's blood. I am giving my evidence".

A HUMOROUS INTERLUDE: Once the Court was the scene of almost riotous laughter, provoked, as is usual, by a chance remark that relieved the tension of a capital trial. The question was whether one of the witnesses could be regarded as morally guilty and unreliable because she had given false evidence before a German Court.

"Isn't it the case," said council, addressing no one in particular, "that occasionally it may happen that false evidence is used to elicit the truth?" "Mais, tous les jours," interpolated the Colonel who presides over the Court-marshal. This cynical avowal of a fact that is, of course, common knowledge coming from such a quarter convulsed the `Court, everyone joining in.

In its bearing on the specific point at issue, whether or not Miss Cavell was denounced by Quien, the evidence was indirect. Quien's attitude was much the same as on previous days. He is cool and collected, seizes on small points that are to his advantage, does not quail before the most terrible accusation, never falters, and is uniformly polite to the President, council, and the most hostile witness.

MLLE. THUILLIEZ'S STORY: When Mlle. Thuilliez stepped into the witness-box she was wearing the ribbons of the

Legion of Honour and the Croix de Guerre. She said she received Quien when he was posing as a French officer. Next day she presented Quien to Miss Cavell. "We wanted," she said, "a man to take people across the frontier. Quien told me he had met such a man, and he presented me in fact to an individual, whom I never saw again. The latter said that he could act as a guide and show where the frontier could be crossed. When Miss Cavell heard the name of the road to which Quien had taken me she said 'That is not a road that you can go into.' I didn't know Brussels. Later on Miss Cavell told me she was very much upset. She had received a small diary, in which Quien had written he had been arrested by the Germans on his return from Holland".

In his dealings with Miss Cavell, witness pointed out, there were several irregularities. Notably after having undertaken to get across the frontiers with the help of the Brussels police he failed to do so, and was found in Brussels when he should have been in Holland. He actually went to Antwerp and on his return from there he asked Miss Cavell to send Mlle. Thuilliez to see him. On two occasions money was given to him, 100 francs by Mlle. Thuilliez and 200 by Miss Cavell. Eventually Quien reached Holland, and on his return was arrested by the German police for having no papers.

HER TRIAL IN BELGIUM: Examination by the Court brought out the fact that Mlle. Thuilliez had every reason that her arrest by the Germans was due to Quien. "In the course of your trial," she was asked, "was there ever a question of Quien?" "Once," she replied. "A police officer of the name of Pinkhoff said to me during the trial: 'Did you not state that you were at the head of the movement with Monsieur de Croy, and then did you not state that you had taken a tall French officer to Brussels?' The fact is that I had never taken any French officer except Quien".

The hearing at this moment was interrupted by Lieutenant Wagner, a Government Commissioner, who expressed to Mlle. Thuilliez the gratitude of the French Government for her heroic conduct, in which Colonel Camus, President of the Court, concurred. Maître Dormon [sic], council for Quien, also expressed his admiration on behalf of the French Bar. Incidentally, it may be mentioned that Mlle. Thuilliez was twice condemned to death by the Germans, her sentence being commuted on each occasion.

POSED AS FRENCH OFFICER: The interrogatory of the witness proceeded, Lieutenant Wagner asking whether Quien had ever spoken to her of acting as a spy. "Yes," she replied, "we had a formal sign with him – HC81". "Did he ever ask you for money?", "Yes, at Mons and Brussels Miss Cavell gave him 300 francs at his request". "How long after he arrived in Brussels should Quien have left?" "Three or four days". Replied the witness. "And as to Quien's conversation in cafés?", "Quien stated at a Mons café that he was a French officer and that he was entrusted with the blowing up of a certain bridge".

She added, in reply to a question for the defence, that after Quien returned from Holland they refused to have anything to do with him. She said that she had told Quien some time before she had ceased to have anything to do with him that he ought not to mix himself up in work such as they were doing, as his abnormal height rendered him too conspicuous.

"Do you say that it was Quien who denounced yourself, Miss Cavell, and others?" asked the council for the prisoner. "It has never entered my mind to accuse Quien," calmly replied the witness, "because I should look upon it as abominable to accuse anyone without proof".

As the result of Mlle. Thuilliez's examination, certain important points were established: first, that Quien definitely offered his services to Mlle. Thuilliez to assist in passing people across the frontier of his own initiative and without authorisation; secondly, that he received money payment, and that from the outset he was aware of the part that Miss Cavell and Mlle. Thuilliez were playing in assisting the fugitives.

PRISONER'S PAST: Mlle. Thuilliez was succeeded in the box by Lambert, a police agent at St. Quentin. His evidence was to the effect that Quien before the war was a recognised scoundrel. Lambert first arrested him for having stolen a motor-car. He had spent money freely at St. Quentin, and passed himself off sometimes as an engineer and sometimes as a barrister. He frequently tried to circulate foreign money, and once, in 1912, when this money was refused he left boxes and papers as security. It became Lambert's duty later to open these boxes, and he found in them packets of 100 mark notes and plans of a dirigible. The is statement created a sensation in court.

Questioned on this point, the prisoner stated that this was quite true, and that he had been interested in a proposed patent dirigible to operate by means of a vacuum. He denied that he had ever had German notes. The matter was not followed up, as the President of the Court pointed out that they were trying Quien on another charge.

AN ENGLISH WITNESS: A friend of Miss Cavell, an English lady named Madame Bodard was the next witness. She explained that they had lodged Quien in Brussels, but were afraid of him. This was after Quien had been taken into the employ of Colonel Desprez (The French Military Attaché), and he tried to get into her confidence by coming from Colonel Desprez and asking her to giver him an account of the money they had expended.

Fearing that her arrest was imminent Madame Bodard made a bundle of some incriminating papers, including some special maps used for crossing the frontier. These Quin was to take to a safe place. Before she knew whether or not he had done so she was arrested, and at her trial before the German court one of these maps was produced in evidence against her.

The next witness was a Belgian named Freyling who had been leader of one of many organisations for getting people across the frontier. Quien came to him, he said, and offered his collaboration. "I found," he said, "after refusing his co-operation that I was being shadowed. Others of my colleagues had a similar experience, and we were all arrested, including Quien. All of us were condemned – myself to death, others to heavy sentences, all but one man, and that (pointing to Quien) was the man in the dock. There is no question he was a German decoy.

He was accused of having been concerned in recruiting with me. I charge him now with having never recruited".

"When before the German court he was indifferent, cynical, mocking, and eventually that Court came to the conclusion that they had nothing against him on that charge. As I say, I was condemned to death, the others to penal servitude. Quien was the only one of us not sent into Germany".

It was elicited that Quien, who swore that he had never seen Freyling, had written to Colonel Desprez . "I was visited by Freyling this morning". Quien's only defence was that he told Colonel Desprez that he had seen Freyling with a view to recruiting him.

MADAME ADAM'S EVIDENCE: Perhaps the most striking of yesterday's witnesses was Madame Adam, whose evidence I have referred to above. She made no attempt to hide her hatred of Quien. He came to her, she said, in distress, and as she could not herself give him a lodging she passed him on, paying for his food and lodging. Eventually she sent him on his way, telling him to visit her aunt and say that he had been sent by 'Ninette', the name she had been known by in her family as a girl. Her people were uneasy at the time and warned her to be careful, and as a result Quien was not taken into their confidence.

"Eventually," she said, "I, my husband, and our child were arrested, and I was asked if my name was Ninette. After ten days I was confronted with Quien. He was asked if he knew me, and he said he did, and that I was the person who had fed him and got him a lodging. As there was no proof against us we were released, but later my three

aunts were arrested. A day before a man had come to their house speaking with a strong German accent and stating that he came from 'Ninette'. As the result of the brutal treatment they received one of them who was ill died.

Following days of evidence, some in camera, *The Daily Telegraph* reported the verdict in the Quien trial, reached on Friday 5th September, under the headline: "*The Betrayer of Nurse Cavell – Sentence to Death – Recommended to Mercy*".

Quien, the betrayer of Nurse Cavell, has been found guilty by the court-marshal and condemned to death. At the same time, six out of the seven members of the Court, on the plea of Maître Darmon [sic], who defended Quien, have signed a petition recommending him to mercy.

When his trial was resumed to-day, Maître Darmon [sic], his council, began his speech for the defence. He had a heavy task, which he discharged courageously. In his speech for the prosecution Lieutenant Wagner had demanded the death penalty for Quien. Before dealing with his powerful arguments showing why the accused man should suffer the death of a traitor, it is necessary, for the purpose of indicating all the evidence produced, to refer again to the documents from Brussels, some of which were mentioned in my yesterday's telegram. Among these was an anthropometric photograph of Quien taken a long time before his arrest. This photograph shows a long and pointed moustache, and it is concluded from this that Quien and the man calling himself Francois Cavier who's description sent by the Public Prosecutor at Brussels resembles somewhat that of Quien as he looks to-day, were not one and the same person. And this contention is further strengthened by the deposition of the secretary of Neels de Roode, who, on being questioned, declared that Neels de Roode had worked with Francois Cavier, who was at the head of a private agency at Brussels before the war, and known to the German police agents, Bergen and Pinkhoff, who frequently visited the office.

Another remarkable document read was the confession of Otto Meyer, the German secret police agent who watched and arrested Miss Cavell. Meyer, who has had an extraordinary career, confessed that when the house of M. Baucq, the architect, was searched, numerous documents which compromised all the members of Nurse Cavell's organisation were found. Quien, said Meyer, in his statement, was not concerned in denouncing Miss Cavell, whatever the French police might say. "Besides," he added, "I know all about him". The reading of Meyer's confession gave great satisfaction to Quien's council, who pressed for more information to support the charge against his client. To this demand, which was rejected by the court-marshal, Lieutenant Wagner replied that he accused Quien of intelligence with the enemy, and that he had never put forward the pretension that he was the sole betrayer of Nurse Cavell.

DEGRADED AND ABJECT: A feature of Lieutenant Wagner's speech for the prosecution, marked by considerable emotion in parts, was the skill with which he limned the portrait of Quien. He had extolled the patriotism of the French, who had suffered under the heel of the Germans. "My task is a painful one," he said, "because I have to ask that another Frenchman be pitilessly dealt with". He described Quien as a degraded, abject man, who with his gifts might have succeeded in life. But to what use had he put his intelligence? To betray. Quien was a swindler, a lazy man, a drunkard, and a débauché who had three occupations – to live well, not to work, and to have mistresses.

The Government Prosecutor proceeded to group the proofs of Quien's guilt – material and mathematical proofs he called them. He dealt with his life from the time when he left saint Quentin gaol to the day when, returning to France through Switzerland, he swindled Madame Mankes out of £60. In order to accuse Quien of intelligence with the enemy it was not necessary to put up against him all the transactions he had with the German police. The affair of Madame Bodart's maps was sufficient, as it afforded "mathematical proof" of his guilt. Madame Bodart had sent five maps to Quien, with instructions that they be sent to Madame Machiels on the same day. Madame Machiels received only three maps. When Madame Bodart was arrested and denied the charges levelled against her, the German judge showed her the maps. They had been drawn by M. Baucq's own hand. There could be no mistake. Quien, who had the packet for more than twenty-four hours, had opened it, taken two maps from it, and handed them to either Pinkhoff or Bergen, both German police agents. With the same clearness the Government prosecutor showed that it was Quien who had denounced Madame Adam, Madame Jacob, M. Ortard, and Mlle. Gauvin at La Louviere.

SEARCHING QUESTIONS: Dealing with the insistence that Quien showed in seeking to obtain from the members of Miss Cavell's institute and exact account of the money spent on fugitives, so that it could be sent to Colonel Desprez, chief of the counter-espionage service in Holland, who would recoup them, Lieutenant Wagner proved that Colonel Desprez had never entrusted him with such a mission. What was the object of the accused? It could be easily guessed. As the supposed agent of Colonel Desprez he had to assist the fugitives in crossing the frontier. Quien, however, never concerned himself about fugitives. It had been presented that he had been wanted by the German police, but he lived in Brussels, and when he was arrested his sentence did not exceed three months. Why was he arrested? So that he could be searched in prison for a note-book containing his memoirs. On this point Lieutenant Wagner asked if it was to be believed that an intelligent man engaged in counter-espionage would have on him a note-book filled with information about Miss Cavell's institute? The note-book was only there to furnish an alibi to the indicator, who was Quien.

Turning to the court-marshal, Lieutenant Wagner concluded: "You must now have the certainty, not that Quien is the exclusive betrayer of Miss Cavell, but that he worked in this affair with the Germans. We have no right by vain sentimentality to insult the memory of all those who died for the country. Remember those heroes at this moment. I demand for Quien capital punishment.

Quien maintained a stolid attitude while Maître Darmon pleaded in his behalf. In passionate language council denounced the murder of Miss Cavell, but pleaded the innocence of his client. He held that no proof had been shown that Quien was responsible for this crime. Further he maintained that Quien was equally innocent of having had intelligence with the enemy. Sketching his client's career, he admitted that while Quien was always in need of money, he invariably applied to French people for it. He argued that if Quien did not return to France, it was because, as he had been promoted to the rank of lieutenant, he would have been reduced to a soldier of the second class. The bad reputation of the accused made his council's task more difficult, but he held that Quien was not a traitor, and that nothing had been established showing his relations with the German authorities.

There is an interesting sequel to the trial which ended on the 5th September 1919. On file is an extract from *The Daily Telegraph* dated 3rd October that same year, in which it states that Quien, the betrayer of Nurse Cavell, whose sentence of death is to be annulled because only four of the judges out of seven voted his condemnation, whereas five votes are necessary, will be re-tried by another court-marshal.

Quien was eventually given a twenty-year prison sentence and served this at Clairvaux. During his term in prison he was regarded as a model prisoner, and it was reported that Brand Whitlock was among those who considered that he was not the actual betrayer of Edith Cavell. United Press, the American agency, reported that Quien had not given up hope of a new trial and that he had continued to protest his innocence. One of his supporters in seeking a review of his case was the prison governor, who commented that Quien's life in prison was "*made 'hell', being shunned by even the lowest felon*".

Quien's release from prison was reported in *The Daily News* in January 1936:

Gaston Quien, a Frenchman who is said to have been the betrayer of Nurse Cavell, has just been released after serving 20 years' imprisonment for espionage on behalf of Germany. According to Le Journal, he says that he is innocent and is preparing documents to prove that he is the victim of mistaken identity.

DETENTION AND TRIAL

SAINT GILLES PRISON

The prison at Saint Gilles was controlled by the Germans, who segregated a part of it to house political prisoners, but continued to leave the day-to-day operation under the control of a Belgian governor and staff. From the outside its appearance was much like a fortress, and its high walls excluded much of the city noise from those held inside.

Louise Thuliez offers a description of the prison:

> *The cells are four metres long, two metres and a half wide, and two metres and seventy-five centimetres high. The window measuring one metre by sixty-five centimetres is placed about one metre seventy-five centimetres from the floor. The upper half is a skylight, opening inwards and from the top so that the prisoner can see nothing whatever of the outside world, not even a glimpse of sky.*
>
> *A folding bedstead that serves the double purpose of a table by day and a bed at night, a wooden stool, a corner cupboard to hold the prisoner's few possessions and a jug with the daily provision of water, that is all.*
>
> *Besides the peep-hole by which the gaoler, going his rounds, can see into the cell without opening the door, there is a wicket through which the prisoner's meals are*

passed to him, and twice nightly the gaolers going their rounds open this wicket and flash the light of their electric torch on the sleeping prisoner's face to see that all is well. It is impossible to describe the disagreeable effect produced by this light suddenly flashing on one's eyes and abruptly awakening one from the delightful, if imaginary, liberty of sleep, back to the harsh reality of prison walls and heavily-bolted doors.

In Belgium the prisoners wear the 'cagoule'. This object is a sort of veil made of rough, greyish-coloured linen; it covers the head and face but has two holes cut in for the eyes. The prisoner is obliged to don this head-dress when for one reason or another he has to leave his cell and meet his fellow-prisoners. . . .

The cell was heated by two hot-water pipes, running along the wall under the window and quite near the floor. These pipes were used by the prisoners as a sort of telephone, the only means they had of communicating with one another. A slight scratching on the pipes, amplified by the sonority of the metal was the signal. Then the prisoners, kneeling each in the corner of his cell, spoke to one another in a low voice through the holes made in the wall for the passage of the pipes. . . .

When the Germans thought fit, the prisoner was authorised to take half an hour's exercise in what we called familiarly the 'cake section'. And in fact, at the extremity of each wing of the prison, there is a round hall with small narrow doors all round it, opening into tiny rectangular gardens, like slices of cake. The triangles are separated one from the other by high stone walls. At the extreme end there is no wall, the space being filled up by heavy iron bars. In the middle of the little garden there is a plot in which some sickly plants are trying to grow. Some of the gardens are also roofed over with iron bars, so that the prisoners who occupy them really feel as though they are in a lion's cage.

During the time allotted for exercise, the prisoner is obliged to walk round and round the cultivated plot in the middle without stopping. There we were narrowly watched, on one side by the officer on guard who surveyed us through the little window cut in the door for that purpose, and on the other, from the barred end of the enclosure, for there was another officer walking up and down outside.

But we still contrived somehow to exchange remarks in low tones with our invisible neighbours. Thus it was that, sharing a garden with the Countess de Belleville I recognised a Lille accent in the garden next to ours and learned that Louise de Bettignies was also a prisoner at St Gilles.

The treatment which Princess Marie de Croy received appears to have been somewhat different to that which Louise Thuliez and others experienced. She was held in what she describes as a 'room', rather than cell, and was given the same food as in the Officers' Mess. She writes of the waiters, Karl and Fritz, who "*wondered at my want of appetite, and recommended favourite dishes, among which I remember was the German delicacy Carpfen*"' and to the two Landsturm men who attended her room.

Louise Thuliez describes the food as sufficient and cleanly-prepared ,although, by German law, they were treated as criminals prior to conviction. This meant very basic food, with meat only twice a week, and no cutlery for the evening meal.

While Louise Thuliez writes that those awaiting trial were not allowed visitors, Marie de Croy was brought fresh linen and news of Reginald's escape by Marie de Lichtervelde. The two women were allowed to speak, in the presence of Lieutenant Bergan, only of family matters and specifically not about the case, except that Lichtervelde was able to confirm that Maître Alexandre Braun would handle her defence. On another visit Marie de Croy heard that a letter which she had previously written to her grandmother had been received. By this time, on the recommendation of a doctor, the two 'Landsturm' men had been replaced by a German 'femme-de-chambre'.

INTERROGATION

The prisoners were questioned by Lieutenants Bergan and Pinkhoff; the former spoke very little French and relied almost entirely on interpreters. Pinkhoff had lived in France for fifteen years before the war and spoke French well, with almost no accent. Bergan played the role of severe interrogator, changing in a moment to sympathetic listener. Pinkhoff, when not with Bergan or interpreters, would attempt to play 'mind games' with the prisoners, leaving them for extended periods of time to confirm or counteract their statements and assertions, pretending to consult with other accused or witnesses. Louise Thuliez wrote of Pinkhoff:

> *An enormous birthmark on the right side of his face, between the eye and the ear, added to the unpleasant impression one had at sight of this brutal visage barred by its heavy black moustache. He always wore a very*

important air, as if on him alone depended the result of the enquiry.

The evidence placed before Louise Thuliez was contained in the dossier prepared by Bergan and Pinkhoff. In it she is identified as entering the home of Philippe Baucq at 49 Rue de Roodebeek, carrying a large parcel. When the police entered the house and interrogated the household, Louise Thuliez initially claimed to be a Madame Lejeune but was later 'obliged to retract'. In her handbag they found a falsified certificate of identity, an address book which could only be deciphered with the aid of a secret code, three notebooks and a number of 'illegal' newspapers.

The evidence against Philippe Baucq was primarily that of him recruiting helpers for the repatriation work and for the printing and distribution of anti German newspapers. The dossier identifies four-thousand such newspapers being found on the premises, many of which had been thrown from the windows by his family when Baucq initially gave the alarm.

The initial case against Edith Cavell seems to have been centred upon a letter, found by Bergan at her clinic in Rue de la Culture, which had been delivered to her via the American Consul in Brussels. The underlying assertion, however, was that Edith Cavell had been a major participant in the escape networks, which used Brussels as the marshalling point for the journey across the border in to Holland and, from there, to repatriation.

Formal statements were taken in French, translated into German by Pinkhoff and typewritten by a clerk, Neuhaus. Later, when asked to sign their statements, written in German, re-translated back into French there were many anomalies which Pinkhoff dismissed simply as translation errors from German into French implying that his German version was an accurate translation of the original. It was the unverified statements in German which were signed.

Although their individual actions were investigated, the main thrust of the examinations was to prove that the accused were part of a co-ordinated network organised by Reginald de Croy. Lists of repatriated English soldiers, their guides and helpers were presented to the accused, and their answers checked and double-checked, one to the other, in an attempt to secure an admission. The Germans were not convinced that Reginald de Croy was no longer available to be arrested on French or Belgian soil, and much of their questioning of his sister was directed towards enabling his capture.

THE TRIAL

The trial of the thirty-five defendants began in secret on the 7th October 1915 in the Belgian Senate building, which was the first that defendants knew for certain who were being similarly charged, having been kept apart since their arrest. There was a five-man panel of military judges, Doctor Eduard Stoeber the Examining Magistrate, Duwe the Clerk of the Court-Marshal and Brueck the interpreter; the last two being German military officers. Also in court were four Belgian lawyers (Maîtres Dorff, Kirschen, Braffort and Braun) and the German lawyer Lieutenant Thielmann. The entire proceedings were in German, with Brueck translating questions into French, and responses back into German.

The six defendants who were charged with the most serious offences were not permitted to hear the evidence and responses of the others, so were removed from the court until it became their turn to be examined. The six excluded were Edith Cavell, Philippe Baucq, Marie De Croy, Louise Thuliez, Jeanne de Belleville and Herman Capiau. The charges against the entire thirty-five accused were: distributing the seditious newspaper '*La Libre Belgique*'; sending messages to enemy soldiers at the front, from their families living in occupied territories; facilitating the escape of soldiers from invaded territories and their return to the front, this last entailing the charge of 'High Treason'.

Edith Cavell was the first to be examined by the court. Both Louise Thuliez and Marie de Croy later wrote of their regret that Cavell chose not to appear in her nurse's uniform, Thuliez saying that the uniform "*would have stood as the emblem of charity and mercy in a place whence all charity and mercy were to be excluded*". Marie de Croy wrote:

> *It was the first time that I had seen her out of nurses' costume, and I think it is a great pity she had not worn it during the trial, as, apart from its charitable significance in all eyes, anything in the way of uniform imposed on the German mind.*

The trial consisted simply of placing before the court a summary of all the questions put to her during the pre-trial interrogations, with no opportunity for her defence lawyer to challenge or elaborate on the prosecutor's assertions and certainly not to examine her before the court. Her sole defence was that she had done what she thought was her duty in saving the lives of men whom she knew were in imminent danger of death.

Second was Louise Thuliez, whose examination followed much the same lines as that of Edith Cavell, except there were questions to her about the organisation of the group and the identification of its chief; the establishment of an organised hierarchy seeming, to her, to be their prime motivation. Asked her motives, Thuliez replied, "*Because I am a French-woman*".

Third to be examined was Philippe Baucq, following a very similar pattern to the previous two, followed by Jeanne de Belleville, Herman Capiau and Marie de Croy. The other accused took their turns until the entire thirty-five had been similarly examined and the defence lawyers had been given an opportunity to make a presentation. After this, Lieutenant Bergan made his assertions that the defendants constituted a single organisation, which worked towards the repatriation of soldiers and men of military age, to join Joffre's big offensive, anticipated by the Germans at that time.

On the second day of the trial the court convened in the Chambre des Députés, rather than the Senate, the proceedings beginning with further summing-up from the prosecutor, Eduard Stoeber. Again, the main thrust was the assertion that the defendants all belonged to a single organisation, with the accusation of High Treason. He concluded by demanding the death sentence for Baucq, Cavell, Thuliez, Séverin, de belleville, Bodart, Libiez and Capiau. The defence lawyers were permitted to make representations, pleading for each of those eight, and each defendant was then allowed to make a statement in mitigation.

When the court rose, there being no need for a verdict, sentences were to be considered, and the defendants were given to understand that they would be communicated to all concerned later on that same day. It was in the afternoon of the third day following the trial that the defendants were gathered together in the central hall of the prison and the sentences given: Philippe Baucq, Louise Thuliez, Edith Cavell, Louis Séverin and Jeanne de Belleville all sentenced to death. On returning to the accommodation block, Louise Thuliez and Jeanne de Belleville were allowed to share a cell, but a request to be joined by Edith Cavell was refused.

On the following morning, 12th October, notice of the court marshal was posted on walls in Brussels. In addition to the death sentences, Herman Capiau, Ada Bodart, Albert Libiez and Georges Derveau were sentenced to fifteen years' hard labour and Marie de Croy to ten years' 'hard labour. Seventeen others were given sentences from two to eight years' hard labour and eight others were acquitted. The final sentence of the notice read, "*Le judgement rendu contra Baucq et Cavell a déjà été exécuté*".

> *The sentence passed on Baucq and Cavell has already been carried out*

EXECUTION

At six o'clock on the morning of 12th October, a small band of nurses was standing outside the gates of the prison of St Gilles to witness two German military cars leave on their way to the Tir National. In one car was Philippe Baucq, in the other was Edith Cavell. The two prisoners were accompanied by a pastor, appointed by the Germans. Paster Paul Le Seur gave his account in a book, *The Truth* by Wilhelm Behrens, transcribed here from http://www.edithcavell.org.uk

> *When we arrived at the Tir National, a company at full war strength (two hundred and fifty men) stood there, in accordance with the regulations, under the command of a staff-officer. A Military Court Councillor, Dr. Stoeber, with his secretary, Capt. Behrens, in command of St. Gilles prison, an officer from the Commander's office, and a medical man, Dr. Benn, were on the spot. We clergymen led the condemned persons to the front. The company presented their rifles, and the sentence was about to be read aloud in German and in French, when M. Baucq*

called out with a clear voice in French: 'Comrades, in the presence of death we are all comrades.' He was not allowed to say anything more. The sentence was read out, and then the clergymen were permitted to have a last word with the condemned persons. I thought I had to make this as brief as possible. I took Miss Cavell's hand and only said (of course in English) the words: 'The Grace of our Lord Jesus Christ and the love of God and the Communion of the Holy Ghost be with you for ever. Amen.' She pressed my hand in return, and answered in those words: 'Ask Mr. Gahan to tell my loved ones later on that my soul, as I believe, is safe, and that I am glad to die for my country.'

Then I led her a few steps to the pole, to which she was loosely bound. A bandage was put over her eyes, which, as the soldier who put it on told me, were full of tears.

Then a few seconds passed, which appeared to me like eternity, because the Catholic clergyman spoke somewhat longer with M. Baucq, until he also stood at his pole.

Immediately the sharp commands were given, two salvoes crashed at the same time — each of eight men at a distance of six paces — and the two condemned persons sank to the ground without a sound. My eyes were fixed exclusively on Miss Cavell, and what they now saw was terrible. With a face streaming with blood — one shot had gone through her forehead — Miss Cavell had sunk down forwards, but three times she raised herself up without a sound, with her hands stretched upwards. I ran forward with the medical man, Dr. Benn, to her. He was doubtless right when he stated that these were only reflex movements.

Indeed, exactly the same physiological process was described in the gruesome murder scene in Oscar Wilde's novel, 'The Picture of Dorian Grey'. Self-control could not go so far, surely, as to prevent a human being in this position from giving a sound if he were still conscious. The bullet-holes, as large as a fist in the back, proved, in addition, that without any doubt she was killed immediately. I only mention this fact because untrue rumours have been connected with it. A few minutes later the coffins were lowered into the graves, and I prayed over Edith Cavell's grave, and invoked the Lord's blessing over her poor corpse. Then I went home, almost sick in my soul.

THE UNITED STATES LEGATION

With no British representation in occupied Belgium, the United States Government, in the person of Ambassador Brand Whitlock, assumed responsibility for protecting the interests of Edith Cavell. Whitlock was unwell on the evening before the executions and it was Hugh Gibson, the Secretary to the US Legation, who acted on his behalf. In his subsequent report to Whitlock he said that he heard of the death sentence on Edith Cavell only that evening, although the German Politische Abteilung assured him that no sentence had yet been passed, that it would be a day or so before any decision was reached and that the American legation would be kept properly informed.

At half-past eight that evening Hugh Gibson learnt from Gaston de Leval, who had himself learnt from Sister Elizabeth Wilkins, that the death sentence had already been passed and that the execution of Edith Cavell would take place during that same night (in fact it took place early the following morning). Gibson and Leval went together to meet with the Marquis de Villalobar, who was dining at the home of Baron Lambert, and the three of them went to visit Baron von der Lancken at the Politische Abteilung with a plea for clemency addressed to the Governor-General.

Although Baron von der Lancken and his entire staff were out for the evening, he returned about ten o'clock when he heard that his visitors needed to see him urgently. Lancken, initially, would not accept that sentence had been pronounced but telephoned the presiding judge of the court-martial, who confirmed that it had, and that it was intended to carry out the sentence before morning. Gibson, Leval and Villalobar pleaded for delay, emphasising the horror of executing a woman, no matter what her offence. They pointed out that the death sentence had previously been reserved solely for actual cases of espionage and that, as she had been for some weeks in prison, a delay in carrying out the sentence could entail no danger to the German cause. They also pointed out what effect such an execution might have on public opinion and counselled the benefits of showing a degree of clemency.

Baron von der Lancken's response was to say that the Military Governor was the supreme authority in such matters and that the Emperor, alone, could intervene. The Military Governor could choose to accept or to refuse an appeal for clemency, and so Lancken agreed to consult directly with him on their behalf but returned later to say that their plea for clemency had been declined.

THE SPANISH AMBASSADOR

The Germans had informed the Marquis de Villalobar that Jeanne de Belleville was a French citizen and was, as such, entitled to be represented by the Spanish Ambassador. Having heard the death sentence, he had telegraphed the King of Spain, requesting that he intercede on her behalf. It was only after this, having been approached by her sister, that the ambassador learnt that Louise Thuliez was also French. It was with some difficulty that Villalobar was able to force the Germans into admitting that they were guilty of a serious diplomatic error in withholding such information. It was not until eight-thirty in the evening of the day following the executions that a telegram was received from King Alphonse XIII and a delay of execution was granted for both Jeanne de Belleville and Louise Thuliez; also for Louis Séverin, a Belgian, whose case was pressed by some "*very influential people*", according to Thuliez.

The German Kaiser was canvassed by Pope Benedict XV and Jules Jusserand (the Belgian Ambassador to the United States) as well as from the United States and, through the Pope, Great Britain. Finally, King Alphonse received confirmation that Jeanne de Belleville, Louise Thuliez and Louis Séverin had all been reprieved and their death sentences commuted to one of hard labour for life; the two women at Siegburg and Séverin at Rheinbach.

PRISON LIFE

Marie de Croy was also sent to Siegburg to serve her sentence, although she says that she never even caught sight of Jeanne de Belleville or Louise Thuliez. The prison regime was very strict, with silence imposed and no communication, verbal or otherwise, allowed between prisoners. Although Jeanne de Belleville travelled immediately to Siegburg, Louise Thuliez was kept in Belgium until a further trial could be concluded in Cambrai; again with interrogations from Bergan and Pinkhoff; again with demands for the death penalty. The sentence was hard labour for life.

Louise Thuliez describes the daily routine of the prison thus:

> *At seven in the morning the getting-up bell brought about a great stir in the prison. Passing rapidly along the landings the wardress opened the cell doors so that we might put out our jug for the daily supply of water and our toilet-pail to be emptied. A quarter of an hour later these articles were given back to us and the doors were locked again until eight o'clock when a meagre allowance of coffee-substitute and one hundred grammes of black bread were served for our breakfast.*
>
> *Ten o'clock was the exercise-hour, one of the moments we most looked forward to in the long day, because we were all together.*
>
> *At half-past eleven work ceased, while soup was distributed and we waited impatiently until it was finished in the hope that there might be a little left over which was always a welcome addition to what had gone before. The absence of bread was very hard to bear at this midday meal.*

> *At one o'clock work began again until darkness fell, only broken by exercise at three o'clock, after which we received some mock coffee again and seventy-five grammes of bread.*
>
> *At six o'clock before the final locking of our cell-doors our evening soup arrived or simply some hot water at our request, for the soup was, more often than not, so nasty that we could not bring ourselves to swallow it. In winter, we had to drink this last beverage as best we could, groping in the dark.*
>
> *At seven-thirty the last bell rang and then, until the following morning, the prison was wrapt in silence, broken only by the wardresses going their rounds at appointed hours and marking their passage on an automatic register.*
>
> *Sunday was a day of rest. We had Mass at nine o'clock and vespers at one-thirty. We were allowed to read then, but the prison library had not been furnished for French readers.*

Her description of the prison regime at Siegburg is quite disturbing to read. The soup was dirty and ill prepared, mostly served with a generous sprinkling of insects. The few scraps of meat which could be detected in the early days of the war were entirely absent by the end of 1916. Women who arrived at the prison with young babies, or gave birth in prison, were too undernourished to feed them. Women giving birth did so quite unaided in their cell. Babies, if they survived, were taken from their mother at nine months old and fostered in the town, being brought to the prison for a brief visit once a month.

Medical aid was virtually non-existent in the prison, little or no medicines available, but also with a complete absence of good-will.

Louise Thuliez particularly quotes the fate of Louise de Bettignies, imprisoned for 'spying' later than the others, who developed pleurisy and was operated on in the infirmary. The conditions and level of care were, at best, rudimentary and her after-care almost non-existent - which resulted in an early death.

The 'hard labour' to which they were sentenced was a day-long activity. Sewing military clothing, embroidering badges or other insignia, manufacturing buttons or otherwise performing housekeeping chores. From breakfast until supper the work was continuous, refusal or slacking in any way meant being shut away in the dungeon. Siegburg was in the midst of munition factories and, at times, the prisoners were set to munitions work which was contrary to the Hague Convention.

FREEDOM

By the end of the war the prison at Siegburg was home to German deserters as well as the regular German criminals and the political prisoners. Mutiny and rebellion was in the air and, on the 8th November, the German prisoners returning from outside day work forced open the prison and released the entire interned population. About six hundred men and women boarded a train for Cologne leaving behind a local population so impoverished that they sacked the prison for the meagre rations that were there.

From Cologne, the French and Belgian political prisoners travelled on to Herbesthal, Verviers, Liège and finally to Louvain. After the Armistice was announced on the 11th November, travel became a little less dangerous but more difficult, in that all trains were then requisitioned by the military. However, the small group finally arrived in Brussels and from there went their separate ways back home.

Marie de Croy's experience was somewhat different. She had been transferred to Clemens Hospital in Münster and learnt of the Armistice from Frau Manser, whom she describes as "*one of the higher officials*". She left Cologne by train, bound for Spa in Belgium, and then on to Louvain. After an enforced delay she finally made Brussels by road and was accommodated by family friends.

The Château de Bellignies was in a sorry state when she finally reached home; the house and grounds had been severely damaged by shelling. The German army having vacated the château, the Allies were then in occupation. She stayed one night at the château and then returned to Brussels.

THE FIRST CASUALTY OF WAR

RMS LUSITANIA

The sinking of the Lusitania by the German submarine U20 was the first major propaganda coup that the Allies were handed. Of nearly two thousand passengers and crew, 1,192 were killed, and although the British government was prepared to condemn Germany for an act of aggression against civilians in time of war, the 128 American deaths enraged President Wilson, his administration and almost the entire population of that country.

The Lusitania had left New York for Liverpool on the first of May 1915 and was about ten miles off the coast of Ireland when Captain Schwieger, the commander of the German U-Boat, fired a single torpedo at the ship and scored a direct hit. A second explosion rocked the Lusitania, and the ship sank within eighteen minutes of the initial attack. It is the second explosion which transposes righteous indignation into British propaganda and which enables the modern reader to view the re-telling of German war atrocities in a more forensic light than they might have done at the time.

Earlier references to Marie Depage identify her as one of the victims of the attack in May 1915. As early as February of that year, Admiral Hugo Von Pohl had declared the waters round Great Britain and Ireland to be a 'war region', and the German Embassy in New York had warned that vessels flying the flags of Great Britain or her allies were liable to be destroyed. Margaret Haig Thomas, a survivor, later wrote:

On Saturday, May 1st (the day on which the Lusitania was to sail), in order that there might be no mistake as to German intentions, the German Embassy at Washington issued a warning to passengers couched in general terms, which was printed in the New York morning papers directly under the notice of the sailing of the Lusitania. The first-class passengers, who were not due on board till about ten o'clock, had still time after reading the warning, unmistakable in form and position, to cancel their passage

if they chose. For the third-class passengers it came too late. As a matter of fact, I believe that no British and scarcely any American passengers acted on the warning, but we were most of us very fully conscious of the risk we were running. A number of people wrote farewell letters to their home folk and posted them in New York to follow on another vessel.

The Lusitania was, in fact, heavily armed and contained a cargo of munitions bound for Britain and her army. The protestations of the British and American governments that the ship was simply a passenger liner, sunk without warning, were simply not true. A second torpedo strike on the Lusitania, as Britain claimed, was really the detonation of the hidden magazine with its secret cargo.

The British government seized upon the sinking to put pressure on the Americans to enter the war against Germany. Newspapers on both sides of the Atlantic were encouraged in their anti-German stance and many of the comments were heavily charged with emotion, such as "*Hun piracy*" and "*Murder on the high seas*". The 'un-defendable' sinking was still very much in the public consciousness when the execution of Edith Cavell was brought to the public's attention later that same year. Brant Whitlock, writing of Edith Cavell's death, refers to the Germans having "*another Louvain, another Lusitania, for which to answer before the bar of civilisation*".

EARLY REPORTS

Early reports of the execution of Edith Cavell in the British press were fanciful in their accounts, encouraged by the propaganda agency based at Wellington House (The British War Propaganda Bureau) in London.

The execution ground was a garden or a yard in Brussels surrounded by a wall. The German firing party of six men and an officer were drawn up in the garden, and awaited their victim. She was led in by soldiers from a house near by, blindfolded with a black scarf. Up to this minute the woman, though deadly white, had stepped out bravely to meet her fate. But before the firing party her strength at last gave out, and she tottered and fell to the ground thirty yards or more from the spot against the wall where she was to have been shot.

The officer in charge of the execution walked to her as she lay motionless on the ground, and, drawing a large service revolver from his belt, took steady aim from his knee, and shot the woman through the head as she lay.

The firing party looked on. The officer quietly returned his revolver to its case, and then ordered the soldiers to carry the body to the house, where charge was taken of it by a

Belgian woman acting under the instructions of the Spanish Minister who had undertaken responsibility for the body, pending arrangements for the burial.

The execution of Miss Cavell has shocked the whole of the Belgian community, who speak of it as the bloodiest act of the whole war.

It is difficult to reconcile this account with that given by Paster Paul Le Seur given in a previous chapter. The myth of the German officer shooting the fallen nurse continued and was graphically portrayed on the picture postcards issued after her death and enthusiastically taken up by soldiers to be sent back to their families at home. Scenes of the 'murder', a description favoured over that of 'execution', show Cavell in nurse's uniform being shot where she lay or else standing facing the firing squad unbound and without blindfold.

One such postcard has, written on the reverse, under her photograph ,"*Miss Edith Cavell, cowardly murdered by a German officer*" and further down, "*Condemned to death by a military tribunal in Belgium, under the charge of having favoured the evasion of British soldiers, Miss Edith Cavell of Norwich, a voluntary nurse, is taken to the execution ground on the 12th of October at day-break. She faints: the german officer gives his soldiers the order to fire, they hesitate to shoot on the prostrate body of a woman. The fiend takes his revolver and leaning upon his victim, deliberately blows her brains out. REMEMBER*".

Patrick J Quinn expresses the view that the execution of Edith Cavell or, more specifically, the fictional account which it inspired, made sure that the British propaganda, developed from the sinking of the Lusitania, was maintained. As Quinn says, of the main conspirators the shooting of a nurse (Cavell) and an architect (Baucq) would serve as a warning to the civilian population without risking the backlash of executing members of the European aristocracy such as Princess de Croy or Countess Jeanne de Belleville. He also claims that America, in the form of Brand Whitlock, became involved, which as a consequence allowed Britain to represent the Americans as being party to the incident. Whitlock's later statement severely compromised America's neutrality.

THE PROPAGANDA MACHINE

Condemnation of the execution became a condemnation of the whole German people and particularly of their moral standing. G K Chesterton was one of the first to share his thoughts, referring to the execution:

. . . it was not done to protect the Prussian power. It was done to satisfy a Prussian power. The mad disproportion between the possible need of restraining their enemy and the frantic needlessness of killing her, is simply the measure of the distance by which the distorted Prussian psychology has departed from the moral instincts of mankind. The key to the Prussian is in this extraordinary fact: that he does truly and in his heart believe that he is admired whenever he can managed to be dreaded. An indefensible act of public violence is to him what a poem is to a poet or a song to a bird. It at once relieves and expresses him; he feels more himself while he is doing it. His whole conception of the State is a series of such coups d'etat.

As early as January 1916, only three months after her execution, an Australian company released a silent movie, *The Martyrdom of Nurse Cavell* although very far removed from the actual story. Emphasis was given to the rebutted attempts by America to save her and the identification of Von Bissing as the implacable German. Australian Prime Minister, William Hughes, was reported as saying that he hoped the film "*may be the medium of impressing on people the dreadful inhumanity of our enemy*".

Even earlier than the Australian film, a book of the same name was published in London with the sub-title, 'The Life Story of Germany's most Barbarous Crime'. Mrs Cavell, at the time of writing, was still alive and living in Norwich and appears to have been the source of much of its content. The book is written in terms of devotion and commitment, of service and piety:

> *It was her gentle way that did most to make me well again . . . I felt she was a minister of God working for my good . . . and there are wounded British soldiers who have pressed the doctors to send them back quickly to the firing line . . . we will go back willingly to avenge this woman's death.*

William Thomson Hill's book is a triumph of popular historical writing with, no doubt, the approval of Wellington House, making references to the "*gallant little Belgian army drawn up across the path of the invaders; the German soldiers ruthlessly slaughtering Belgian women and children*"; "*Nurse Cavell was an Englishwoman - that, was the beginning of her offence*". The early press account of her swooning and, lying on the ground in her nurses uniform, being shot at point blank range is repeated. "*Before the day dawned her body was laid to rest in the land occupied by her enemies, whom with her last breath she forgave*".

Hill employed every element of patriotic fervour available: a wreath of laurels placed by Nelson's Column amongst those of the sailors who had died for England, whilst Nelson himself looked down on the memorial of a weak woman who had borne witness to his immortal message: the men who fought at Trafalgar welcoming her to their company and, in her death, the true spirit of England leaping into life.

Arthur Winnington-Ingram, the Bishop of London, was reported to have said that the death of Edith Cavell would ensure enough willing recruits as to make compulsion unnecessary. Hill writes that recruiting meetings were held in Trafalgar Square all day long and that "*men competed in their eagerness to join the army*".

However, the Cavell effect was short-lived, by January 1916 conscription for single men had to be introduced and, within a few months, was extended to include married men.

HOME FROM THE WAR

On the 17th March 1919 the body of Edith Cavell was exhumed from the 'Tir National' rifle range, where it had been buried by the Germans. Two months later it was transported by rail to Ostend and from there was taken by HMS Rowena to Dover, then by special railway carriage to London on May 15th, accompanied by members of the Cavell family. A horse-drawn gun carriage took the coffin through spectator-lined streets

to Westminster Abbey and a very prestigious funeral service, attended by George V.

The government had expressed the view that she should be buried in Westminster Abbey, but the family decided that Norwich would be more appropriate. Edith Cavell was carried by train from London to Norwich, and then by gun carriage to Norwich Cathedral, where she was interred outside the south transept and where her memorial now stands. Other memorials were erected, the two most notable being in London and Brussels, the latter dedicated to her and Marie Depage.

CONCLUSION

Without doubt, Edith Cavell was a remarkable woman, and much has been written of her dedication and of her religious beliefs, which she followed in both principle and action. In life she was admired and in death she was lauded, as much for having been executed as for having helped Allied soldiers. Her reputation was made by the propaganda machine at Wellington House, a reputation entirely warranted, portraying Edith Cavell as the war hero that saved many from death or incarceration.

In reality, it was a disparate group of individuals which defied the Germans, repatriated Allied soldiers, nursed the injured back to health and gave hope to the families of soldiers trapped far from home. This was not an organisation in the normal sense of the word, but a loose network; there was not a leader or a central committee, but there was a small number of men and women who formed the backbone of the group and co-operated in a common cause. Edith Cavell was central to the operation, but there were others, almost forgotten now, who risked their lives on a daily basis, lived rough in the forest, smuggled men and information through enemy lines and put their own families in mortal danger from German revenge. Louise Thuliez, Henriette Moriamé and René Delame number among these.

The war was fought in the grip of a class system to which we are no longer bound. The social differences between officers and men were evident in both armies and were mirrored in the population at large and in the resistance movement. Without doubt the leaders were the Prince and Princess de Croy and the aristocratic de Belleville family, and it was these that were automatically recognised by the restored government of Belgium at the end of the war; the rest were granted their honours and recognition upon others' suggestion.

READING LIST

History of the Great War, W Stanley Macbean Knight, Caxton Publishing Company, 1914

Edith Cavell, Diana Souhami, Quercus, 2010

War Memories, Marie Croy, Macmillan & Co, 1932

Belgium and the Monarchy, Herman Van Goethem, Asp / Vubpress / Upa, 2010

With Edith Cavell in Belgium, Jacqueline Van Til, H W Bridges, 1922

The Outbreak of the First World War, David Stevenson, Macmillian Press Ltd, 1997

The Long Silence, Helen McPhail, I B Tauris & Co Ltd, 1999

The 'German Atrocities' of 1914, Sophie de Schaepdrijver, Penn State University

The Secret Press in Belgium, Jean Massart, E P Dutton & Company, 1918

Condemned to Death, Louise Thuliez & Marie Poett-Velitchko, Methuen & Co, 1934

German Terror in Belgium, Arnold J Toynbcc, George H Doran Company, 1917

The National Archives, Catalogue reference: KV 2/844

1914: Voices from the Battlefields, Dr Peter Liddle, Mathew Richardson, Pen and Sword Military, 2013

Valenciennes. Occupation Allemande 1914-1918, René Delame, Imprimerie Hollande Fils, 1933

A Noble Woman, Ernest Protheroe, The Epworth Press - J Alfred Shar, 1916

Source Records of the Great War, Vol. II, ed. Charles F. Horne, National Alumni 1923

This Was My World, Margaret Haig Thomas Mackworth, Macmillon and Company 1933

The Conning of America, Patrick J Quinn, Costerus, 2001

The Martyrdom of Nurse Cavell, William Thomson Hill, Hutchinson, 1915

The Case of Miss Cavell, Ambroise Got, Hodder and Stoughton, (date unknown)

www.ingramcontent.com/pod-product-compliance
Ingram Content Group UK Ltd.
Pitfield, Milton Keynes, MK11 3LW, UK
UKHW041828200726
13854UKWH00002BA/879

9 781909 465381